A Housewife's Guide to Women's Liberation

A Housewife's

Women's

Guide to Liberation

Elizabeth Anticaglia

Nelson-Hall Chicago

ISBN 0-911012-69-9

Library of Congress Catalog Card No. 72-85884

Manufactured in the United States of America

Dedicated
to
Jeannine and Jason

Contents

Preface

Last summer, I was invited to participate in a series of Sunday seminars at the Unitarian Church. Knowing that Unitarians are traditionally a literate, liberal group of people, involved in community and world affairs, and active in current phenomena, I collected data and statistics and arrived on my Sunday clutching a fistful of index cards crammed with figures, percentages, and quotations. I was going to be well prepared for questions on court decisions, labor problems, university discrimination, philosophical trends —in short, all the questions of any group wanting to be up on the latest information.

I never used my information. During the discussion period which followed my talk, I was asked only the most basic questions from this highly educated audience—questions like: "Isn't it true that women must take off from work a few days every month?" and "Doesn't every woman really want to be a mother before anything else?"

That was when I decided that the literature now available on feminism was not filtering down past the New York editorial clique. These people certainly recognized the names of Germaine Greer and Kate Millett; they knew Betty Friedan had written *The Feminine Mystique,* and they knew that feminists were trying to "change the abortion laws." But aside from this, they were naive on the subject of feminism. They wanted very much to get further into the Women's Liberation movement and learn exactly how it related to them.

These people were frightened and threatened by this mushrooming movement, yet they realized that it is the "Movement of the Seventies." As with-it people, they wanted to understand it. But it hits home harder than black, ethnic, or Chicano power ever will —and Unitarians, like everyone else with set rules for living, were threatened.

Today, Women's Liberation is one of the top ten discussion topics at any cocktail party, and probably Number One in most women's minds. Yet the literature is geared for college graduates, scholars, "professional feminists," and perhaps politicians. Though a movement bound to affect every person, it has neglected the "average American."

I decided to write a book that will clear away the distortions and misconceptions that surround the feminist movement. In a year of speaking to groups, from high school organizations to women's clubs, I have found a great yearning to learn more, to understand, and to get beyond the media propaganda about feminism. I felt a book tackling every issue as it relates to the housewife (including the one who works and the budding housewife), written in a lively, close, nonintellectual way, was needed.

So many of these women tell me after my talks, "I agree with many things the feminists are saying, but I just can't go along with the aggressive attitude." My book is for them—to show why the aggressive attitude is necessary, and why even this unfavorable image is beneficial.

My book is for the woman who loves her family, but cannot feel completely at home with the domestic role. She needs something more. I feel the first step is to raise her awareness.

My book is for the woman who is educated through high school, perhaps even college, but is not ready to tackle Kate Millett or Lucy Komisar. She can relate to Sue Kaufman's "mad housewife" and to Judith Viorst. The time has come for a feminist book just for her.

The benefits she can derive here involve information—not facts and figures to be forgotten but principles about issues, so she can discuss abortion, day care, woman's body, *Playboy,* and *Ms.* with meaning, because her answers are from her own life. This will be a book she can refer to for more specific information as the movement evolves. It will, most of all, be a means to consciousness-raising in viewing advertising, TV serials, reading materials—to awaken her to the sexism in our society.

This book is by a housewife, a mother, and a writer and is talking to another housewife-mother, another woman. It is not a philosophical, sociological thesis; it is not radical or underground. It is highly personal. I discuss my own awareness, my husband and children, my friends, and my attitudes. And, finally, it delves into all aspects of feminism, from history to biology, from cosmetics to morality. I do not give answers, but I hope I offer the road to solutions.

I wish to express my gratitude to the many people who helped in the writing of this book, and to thank especially my consciousness-raising group for their great enthusiasm, love, and encouragement, and Dr. Robert Bell, Professor of Sociology, Temple University, Philadelphia, for generously providing information and advice.

Prologue:
The Masculine Mystique

The other morning, one of the television talk shows featured a "frank, adult discussion" of female frigidity, starring several authorities. The fact that these "experts" were all male is not unusual; actually, it's traditional. The male sex is very free about discussing not only female frigidity but female orgasm and sex desires; men tell women how to give birth "naturally," how to nurse their babies, and how to bring up their children. Historically, men have been the experts in educating women on how to be women.

And yet, presumptuous as it seems, here I am, another man, introducing a book written for women, about women, and by a woman. But the recurring theme of this work affects every one of us—male and female. This theme is the blatant neglect of half of humanity.

Almost without exception, society has shackled woman into a dependent role, thus preventing the maximization of her full potential. An overstatement, you say? Well, let us examine it for a moment.

For centuries, the patriarchal system of civilization has placed man as its standard and woman (in the term of Simone de Beauvoir) as the "other." This system evolved its own male-oriented definitions for the human race, using, in fact, "man" as the synonym for human; "mankind" for humanity; "history" to tell *his* story; and "He" when referring to God.

Matriarchies have existed, but women, in general, possessed little real power in such societies. The label "she" evolved to signify objects of support, such as the ships that carried men over the oceans. Deprecation of women grew through the ages. The male orthodox Jew thanked God in daily prayer for not making him a woman. The ancient Greek and Roman cultures esteemed the male virtues of skill, force, and daring: it was acceptable for the Roman man to commit adultery; however, a Roman woman did so at the risk of "justifiably" losing her life. The early Christians went even further by usurping the woman's role as sole life-giver and nurturer; the Christian infant did not receive an immortal soul, or life, until he was baptized and became a child of the male God.

As the patriarchal system chiseled out guidelines for civilization, woman sank deeper into the quagmire of second-class citizenship. Politically powerless, intellectually starved, and spectators in art and religion, woman had little option but to beget and nurture children. Therefore, this was accorded to be her nature and her essence. It was "unnatural" for her to open the kitchen door to pursue another role.

Today, one must examine this "maternal instinct," or the innate ability of any woman to be an expert in dealing with the needs of the offspring. According to Una Stannard, women have not shown much inborn tendency to cherish, nurture, or protect children. "It is estimated that in the mid-eighteenth century 74.5 percent of all children died before they were five years old. They had always died in such great numbers and disease was not the chief killer; it was maternal ignorance and neglect. The 'maternal instinct' had taught women to feed newborn infants such foods as butter, black cherry water and roast pig. They then dipped the babies in cold water and wound them tightly in swaddling bands, which were not changed more than once a day (if that often), for it was believed that changing and washing babies 'robbed them of their nourishing juices.' Restless babies were fed opium and alcohol."

Yet, this myth of "maternal instinct" persists alongside the other fictions concerning women. One must analyze the misogynists of the nineteenth century in attempting to flash some light on the reasons for the neglect of women in history. Middle-class nineteenth century attitudes were projected into the twentieth century by the writings of Schopenhauer, Nietzsche, and especially Sigmund Freud, who boldly characterized man as the human "norm" and woman as "deficient" man. The patriarchal system reached its zenith under Freud's influence by using psychoanalysis to reinforce age-old prejudices against women.

Freud assigned to women a subordinate role and argued that female inferiority has its basis in the realization by a girl that her brother or male playmate has a penis, which she is denied. All she possesses is a "wound," as Freud characterized her genitalia. Not only does the girl envy her brother, but she begins to share the male contempt for her own sex. Her subsequent behavior is influenced by this male envy and female condescension.

But a woman can overcome her "penis envy," Freud continued, by giving birth to a male child, thus acquiring a penis. Balderdash? Yet, the only Freudian who rejected this thesis was Alfred Adler, who stated that a woman's situation is more influenced by society than biology.

Biologically, differences certainly exist between the sexes. And Ashley Montagu gives evidence showing the female to be physically superior to the male. Be that as it may, differences between the sexes do not imply deficiencies. Distinctions exist as to sex hormones, genitalia, and one's role in reproduction and nursing capabilities. At issue is whether such distinctions characteristically affect a person's behavior.

Overwhelming evidence supports the view that society molds a person's behavior. Biological differences have little, if any, significance in terms of the thoughts, feelings, and attitudes of the average individual. Masculinity and femininity perforce must be reduced to the reproductive differences between the sexes. The higher status men hold in society today is not supported by any scientific evidence of superior abilities unique to men.

Surprisingly, the oppressive three Ks that define a woman's role—Kuche, Kirche, and Kinder—still have devotees in this society. The following pages will challenge the legitimacy of the three Ks. Hopefully, they will provoke in women the question, "How am I going to fulfill my potential *before* the children are grown?"

This doesn't mean that as men we are no longer necessary. However, just as women are now defining themselves and their own situations, men must also find their own individual definitions as well, going beyond the historically male traditions of violence and supremacy. The result will be the discovery that we are all human beings first, and male or female second.

JOSEPH R. ANTICAGLIA, M.D.

1

Who Took Femininity

Out Of Feminism?

"Bitch, Sisters, Bitch!"

"Protest the mindless boob girlie symbol of American womanhood. Help crown a live sheep Miss America. Burn bras, fashion magazines, and cosmetic goop in a freedom trash can."

"Marriage means rape and lifelong slavery."

"Women's International Terrorist Conspiracy from Hell."

"No more fun and games." (That's the one that bothers me. I like fun and games, especially with men!)

The Feminist Movement. Slogans like these certainly don't sound typically feminine, do they? Webster says *feminine* implies weakness, gentility. The feminists today are hardly gentle and most certainly not weak.

But let's look at the opposite end of the spectrum—the Pussycat League. Their mottoes run: "The lamb chop is mightier than the karate chop" and "Why make points when you can make nice-nice?"

Kind of nauseating, isn't it?

The issues being raised here are vital. What is a woman's role today? Does she even have a role? What is expected of a woman, and what has she traditionally expected from herself? Very little, I'm afraid. Up to now.

Today, millions of women are stepping forward to plant their feet firmly on some turf between the Pussycats and the Tigers. What they want is called *liberation*. What they demand is *equality*.

Today, equality has taken on a terrifying meaning, having been tied, in some way, with unisex. *Equality* does not mean *identity*. It does not imply that women want to be the same as men—that is ridiculous and impossible. Nor does equality mean trading the conventional domestic female role for the bread-winning male role. Exchanging roles with men would only result in new oppressive roles for everyone, and that is just what feminists do *not* want.

What equality really means is freedom of choice, a chance at the smorgasbord of alternative life activities —a bit of this, a slice of that—activities to fit one's own life-style and needs. Therefore, equality is, at its very basis, freedom from preconceived attitudes of what "femininity" and "masculinity" mean.

For one woman, the new choice may be complete domesticity; for others, the choice might be to become a physician or an architect, to marry or to remain single. That freedom, that equality, that choice does not exist today. But tomorrow it will. What is it going to mean? That's what this book is about.

Admit it. You suspect there is more to the "good life" than seeing your face reflected in a freshly rinsed dish. You love your husband; you enjoy your children; but all too often you feel your contributions to family life are taken for granted. In ever-increasing moments, you realize that the domestic role has been slipped on with the wedding band, until death do us part. At some point in life, every woman asks herself, "Does being born female mean being born servile?"

Maybe you're a career girl and you feel that, while secretarial work isn't your idea of glamor and accomplishment, it's the fastest road to wherever you're heading. It offers the best pay, a chance to meet men, and a place to kill time until the prince of your dreams brings you to life with marriage.

Or you have a teenager in your home, and you learn that she doesn't want to study nursing or social work, and can't see herself teaching, yet you want her to go to college and prepare for a vital career. What's left for a girl in a society where there aren't many practical "feminine" fields with doors swinging open to her?

Everything is not right in the world of women. Countless times we've all sighed "It's a man's world," but today's women are really questioning it with a booming *Why should it be?* Who was it anyway that ruled, when a family goes picnicking, mother must prepare lunch while daddy grabs a snooze? Who convinced us that only men slave all week and deserve a break? Who argued that women never had it so good, intimating that it doesn't have to get any better? And who was it that claimed women can be secretaries but not executives, kindergarten teachers but not university professors, sandwich makers rather than decision makers. It wasn't contemporary woman who said that. Not even a Pussycat.

You may agree with much of what I'm saying here, but those marching damsels who blare their slogans on television still turn you off, don't they? In fact, you are kind of embarrassed at their harsh unhappiness. It's just not *you*.

"Frustrated lesbians!" you mutter, snuggling into your safe, if not stimulating, sofa corner.

Or, if you're more decorous, "How freaky!" followed by, "I know I'm liberated. That's *their* problem."

But is it only "their" problem? Sorry, but no, it's not. Every woman on our little planet is in the same situation. We do live in a man's world. Men run our political and cultural life; they dictate the clothes we wear and the make-up we apply. Men film the movies we watch, and they write our history books. In short, men tell women what it takes to be womanly. We learn to distrust each other for the favor of men. Later, we teach our daughters to play the same game. Read on—you'll see what I mean.

Maybe the tactics of radical "libbers" are not your style, but deep down there is a hard kernel of truth to what they're wailing, and you'll find that kernel—that tiny grain at the crux of this tremendous and often frightening Women's Liberation Movement.

This book is a guide to your liberation, as a housewife, career woman, parent. It will help you find that truth which relates to *your* life. No matter how sick of and embarrassed by the strident set you are, there is some point of identification for you, and when you find it, you can start digging through the mythology that has clouded something we all share as women—femininity. This doesn't mean your world is going to fall apart; rather, it means that you, as a woman, are going to step into the world. Not the snuggling-bunny world of feminity sold in magazine ads, but the real, throbbing, stimulating world of NOW!

Yes, this is a book for women's rights, one that is going to try to treat this whole controversial and irreversible trend in a sensible, down-to-earth manner, a way most women—average, everyday women like us—can accept as something that pertains to them and their lives. Why? Because the women's movement is fundamentally a plea to apply human rights to women. Blacks, Indians, and Chicanos are battling against discrimination, so now women are resuming their fight, one they have dropped and picked up sporadically through the centuries.

Unfortunately, an unsavory slant has been given the Movement. Newspapers and television shows are copy hungry. What they are pushing is titillation, not truth; controversy, not consideration. After all, it is more fun to watch angry, man-hating females scream their war cries than to listen to intelligent, thought-provoking statements by concerned and intellectual women such as Kate Millett. Dispute brings out the "ha-ha" side of men; brawling evokes fun-poking; so how can you protest when those women don't appeal to you any more than they do to your husband?

"I can see all that," you agree. "But why *do* they have to fight? It's so unfeminine."

Every woman knows the answer to that. If you are apathetic and let people take advantage of you, they will do just that. If you allow the butcher to give you fatty bottom round when you asked for lean top round, he will slip it to you. If *you* don't care, why should *he?* It is a fact of American life, perhaps of human life everywhere, that until someone raises a ruckus, sometimes a violent one, business continues as usual: for example, manufacturers will continue to pollute our environment and to sell us nylon stockings that run much too easily and high-cost appliances with short-life expectancies. And we will continue to live by standards of what is feminine defined by those who are masculine. Unless we complain!

Isn't it our right as women and as human beings to demand and receive, wherever possible, the best we can get and the highest we can achieve? That is what Women's Liberation is about—our human rights.

In this book we're going to examine how we've been programmed into second-class citizenship. We're going to look at the ways, historical and contemporary, that the manipulators of our society work to keep women down, physically and mentally. And by the time you reach the final page, you're going to demand your rights too. How do I know? Because, as a woman, I don't underrate you; I don't relegate "the power of a woman" to standing behind some masculine throne.

No matter how ungracious the problems appear across the "tube," we are all discriminated against as females. Maybe you are now so used to it that you don't even notice anymore; perhaps you've forgotten all the little steps leading to the grand whitewash—the digs, the put-downs, the myths you now accept as truths.

We are so used to thinking of ourselves as "women" (and one-dimensional at that—either domestic or sexual) that we fail to realize that we are actually multifaceted people. For example, you have the same grey matter between your ears as your husband has, yet when you invite your neighbors over for a drink, you sense that the men tune you out. You are not a valuable conversationalist. Little flirtations men love, but let a woman bring up the latest presidential caper and a mask drops over her male companion's face, a mask that features a smug smile. Nothing intellectual allowed from the "little woman" next door.

So, dismiss what you're *supposed* to be and discover what you *are*. Without a psychiatrist (we hope).

"Why bother?" you say. "I like things the way they are."

"I can get what I want from my husband; we women have our ways."

"I've never felt shackled."

"I don't want to be drafted. I don't want to work with a jackhammer. I want to be cuddled and protected."

"No one forced us into marriage. We chose it."

I hear you saying all these things. Forget them.

They're beside the point. More important, they're not even true.

Maybe your whole being *is* geared toward serving your family at your own expense, but even if it is, you won't lose anything by examining your life to find out if you really are completely satisfied with your existence as it is now—if things could not be better for you without a complete upheaval. Perhaps you are coddled and protected, secure in your home, happy with your children, and you wouldn't have it any other way. That's fine. If this is where it's at for you—enjoy, enjoy. Still, it won't hurt you to find out. Then the decision truly will have been yours. Right now, it is society's.

The trend today is toward women working at something else besides housework. Fifty-five percent of childbearing-age women are working full time outside the home, and you may become one of them—if not soon then perhaps in the future. Just what your part will be, I don't know; *you* may not know.

Society has suffocated us, confused us, told us what to be like, and what to want for ourselves—but according to everyone else's needs. We women have traditionally been instruments of service, paragons of the Madonna-seductress—demure on the one hand, sexy on the other. In times of war, we are urged to go out and work; in peacetime, to stay home!

It is important to recognize that your satisfaction ultimately depends upon you—no one else. You must be selfish to be unselfish. You must respect yourself. Until you do, no one else can respect you.

You say you *are* respected. Your *husband* respects you. Maybe he does, but respects you for what reasons?

He says you're a prize of a housekeeper, a devoted wife, a good lover—what he means is you've lived up to *his* standards, and satisfied his needs. But a competent hired girl could take care of most of those needs; and for the rest, a mistress. Of course, the price would be higher—far higher.

You say your *children* esteem you. If you're honest and if you know what's going on around you, you certainly won't say that. You've brought up your children, and it's a laudable, all-consuming job. But when it's over, children remember their *parents*. If they get into trouble, mother and father are to answer for it. If they turn out creditably, again, mom and dad share applause. In other words, even if you've spent twenty-four hours a day for eighteen years caring for your children, you split the rewards with your husband.

But, you say, *you* respect yourself. Well, let's see. You claim you're everything you want to be, but do you keep up with the world by reading the newspapers regularly? And peruse all the best books? Do you take adult education courses to keep your mind in gear; look casually chic all the time; and keep your house in a constant state of readiness for those friends who like to "drop in"? For your rising businessman, are you a gourmet cook and a poised hostess? Never cranky? A patient, loving, Ginott-reading mom—all the time?

Do you know the subtleties of love-making, and are you always seductive to your husband (but demure towards other men)? And are you a fine human being, showing true compassion for those less fortunate, even if they're grimy or vulgar?

You score perfect on all these points, right?

Wrong. Of course, you don't. These are parts of the impossible goal our society has made women feel they should achieve.

Okay, you admit that something may be wrong with our society and the role we women have to play in it, but how could you face your friends if you said you were for "Women's Lib"? What would they think?

First, try to put all that out of your mind for now. Remember, everything Betty Friedan, Germaine Greer, and Gloria Steinem say does not apply to every woman in the world. Just as men differ about their vocations, women vary regarding their destinies. The road to Women's Liberation, according to this housewife, is not one specific road that all women must travel. Rather, it is a route with many alternative paths. It is a hope.

Your primary liberation aim will be different from mine. Mine may be seeing that child-care centers are available for all children, regardless of whether or not their mothers work outside the home. Yours may be returning to school full time for a college degree. Or it might be remaining a housewife — with a few choice sidelines (by "choice," I mean your choice).

Forget, also, about no cosmetics, straight hair, and frumpy clothes. Once you find out what you are, you can come to your own decision about how you want to look, as well as act and live. The world needs you— your brains, your complexities, your special talents, your contributions. And you need to donate yourself.

Your first step in liberation is seeing the world through feminist eyes, raising your consciousness, awakening yourself to the false images that, for centuries, have been dangled before you. The next step is learning how to *want* to develop your capabilities to the fullest. This book will help you see the way.

We fifty-three percent of the American social scene are valuable components of our culture, and we'd better start appreciating ourselves as whole individuals, rather than as cardboard mothers, wives, or sex objects. Day in and day out, we are expected to provide tasty food, a pleasing home, clothing, and emotional support for our families. We have in our solidarity an enormous potential for changing what is wrong in this land and in this world. But, to accomplish, we don't have to overwhelm. We don't have to charge into combat against what many Sisters call "the enemy." Men don't have to be the enemy. They need liberation too.

In a *feminine* way, then, we can muster *all* that is in us to make this a better world for ourselves and for our children. I want to emphasize two words from this last sentence. The first is *feminine*. This is not to mean cajoling, batting eyelashes, and promising sex to get your way, which is degrading to an adult woman. We are too important for that. By feminine, I mean "gently, yet tenaciously."

On the other hand, we must not dismiss determination. Who says aggressiveness is solely a masculine trait? Look at a two-year-old girl in dirty blue jeans crunching through autumn leaves as robustly as any two-year-old boy. We women are complex. We still have vestiges of that little girl within us. That is not to say we have to act like men when we are mature. Who wants that? In male hands, the world has witnessed enough violence. Still, history has proven that at times progress and tolerance stand still until some turbulence prods it into new action. Our battling Sisters have brought this issue to the forefront for the rest of us to cope with in our own ways.

The other word is *all—all* that is in us. For ages now we have been taught that the only "natural" attitude in women is one of subservience. "Them days are gone forever"—and good riddance. This is the Age of Action, and the world will be the better for it.

Modern woman is a special breed, hesitating between a familiar yesterday and a threatening tomorrow. She sees the world changing and is no longer content to passively rock some mythical cradle.

Yet, if we don't want to scream and yell, what can we do? Most of us don't really believe that when a woman marries, husband becomes lord and master while wife becomes the lowly maidservant. We are beyond that. Yet we cling to this cruel game of betraying ourselves in return for some sort of protection. We have all heard how we are physiologically more resilient than our men, yet we pretend to be the weaker sex. Why? Is it easier that way? Is it convenient to pretend to need chivalry?

Incidentally, chivalry is not all that rampant. I recall that when I rode the New York City subway to work in my premarital days, the men who shared the same sardine space were anything but Prince Valiants —more like King Crudes. Hardly ever was I offered a seat by a man; seldom was an elderly lady or a pregnant woman given a seat. Of course, some older gals caught on and became, unwittingly, the forerunners of today's militant feminists, for no one could beat them once their eyes lit upon an empty seat. Umbrellas flying, arms flailing, these hardly-gentle dames fought hand-bag and laced shoe to get that empty seat. And they did—through force, just like contemporary feminists battled to get into a men's saloon.

What I'm getting at is that chivalry is dying, yet we pretend it flourishes. Naturally, men play the chivalry game too, but why shouldn't they? They have everything to gain by doing so. Since we lost our so-called protective advantages long ago, why do we keep on with this sham?

I well remember taking my first halting steps into the world of Women's Liberation. It was at the first meeting of a local chapter of one of Philadelphia's major women's rights groups. About eight women were present when I entered, and I glanced around, looking for raised fists, buttons, and straggly hair.

And they were all looking at me.

There we were, the most housewifely gathering you could find anywhere—perfect examples of the suburban, middle-class stereotype. However, we all had faced the realization that something was awry in our lives: nothing uproarious—no shattered marriages, no trauma or turmoil—just a feeling of desperation over our place in the world. And we wanted to do something about it—not march in the streets, storm into men's clubs, or scream obscenities—but something.

We gathered in the living room of a small, colonial, brick house in the suburbs and tried to sound each other out, and to express why we were here instead of at home, where we could be catching up with the ironing, fixing tomorrow's casserole, or rolling up our hair. Instead, daddy was home baby-sitting, in several cases, very reluctantly. We were all out to be "liberated" and somehow it was funny, until, one by one, we began to express how much liberation meant to us.

"This is my first step toward liberation," a fortyish matron began, "just coming here, when my husband is so against it. Maybe it's not such a big step," she added, apologetically.

We had all spent our lives revolving around our husbands and this breaking away against their wishes was kind of hazardous.

"I now use Ms. on all my correspondence, instead of Mrs.," another housewife offered. She was obviously more advanced than the others. "After all, my husband uses Mr. just as he did before we were married, so why shouldn't I find some way of expressing the fact that it should not matter if I'm married or not?" She added, "Of course, since I'm not working, the only time I have to use it is in sending checks."

Since a weekend meeting of a national Women's Liberation group was coming up, a paper was sent around the room for signatures of those who wanted more information. No one signed.

"I'd love to go," spoke the hostess, "but I just can't hurt my husband's feelings. He got used to the idea of meetings like this one, but for me to spend a whole weekend away . . . anyway, he hasn't been feeling well lately."

Things were not so funny anymore. Here were nine women, moved enough to investigate their lives for meaning, yet they were threatened. Women's Liberation is no joke to women like these. They were taking a risk and a certain amount of action.

During the coffee break, a young mother of four leaned over to confide, "This is my first try at one of these meetings, and you know what? I didn't even know what was the right thing to wear!"

"I wasn't sure if I should put on perfume," I admitted.

The problem of what to wear to a Women's Liberation meeting, like the midi dispute, was solved the same way by each of us—we all wore pants suits!

So you see, the battle for women's rights is not so alien or forbidding, is it? It starts off with a group of sensitive housewives who are in the first grade of self-appraisal. It continues with a commitment, a resolve to meet the following month and to begin a practical project—speaking to other housewives, reading the emerging feminist literature, complaining to local discriminatory employers, writing letters to offensive advertisers. And, in my case, writing a book for other sensitive housewives—a book in which I could share with you my own growth and point out that *femininity* has always been in *feminism;* it's just that the sexist manipulators in politics, business, and communications have been "scribbling" over the word, obscuring its true meaning.

Hopefully, we will be spurred on to examine these words and to look into ourselves—to get to know our bodies a lot better, and to give our minds a lot more credit. From then on, who knows where we'll go. And where our daughters will go!

2

Advertising
and Our Insecurities

When television slaughtered Richard Nixon in 1960 only to successfully sell him eight years later, we learned that TV is the high-quota pitchman of all time. Television plays lots of roles—baby-sitter, entertainer, potential educator—but its favorite role is salesman, and its number-one product is American womanhood.

TV sells womanhood by wrapping it with guilt. Commercials work creatively—and all too successfully—to convince us of what deplorable wives and mothers we are, and consequently, what miserable failures at femininity.

Have you ever noticed how perfect those advertising housewives are? They never lose their cool. The kids scream, spill milk, act rude; birthday parties are bedlam; husbands leave their used bologna packages open—yet these wives and mothers react by smiling complacently, with understanding, and then they give a saucy shake of their well-coiffed heads and start right in cleaning up, or baking a cake, or playing leapfrog in the backyard.

As a wife and mother, I am a FLOP, spelled with capital letters. At least according to TV.

I don't think I could take it if my son lashed out at me for losing his favorite ski sock, or if my daughter tossed her laundry at me to iron "right now," even if she did make everything okay again by admitting that she noticed the "springtime" smell. And if some teeny-bopper came to me and cooed that she hopes her hands look as young as mine when she's my age, I think I'd wrap that plastic bottle of dishwashing detergent right around her neck.

Television commercials can make you neurotic. I know. When I was first married, I practically begged for the solution to my problems that I knew these TV women would eventually offer me. Let's make that "solutions," since every commercial offers a different placebo.

First there is the medical answer: When the kids' raptured squealing turns into screaming, pop two pills, and by the time hubby drives in from work, the children will be placidly pajamaed, and you, all primped for an evening of discothequing. (Advertisers' couples love to go out on wild, late, weekday soirees; don't they have mornings to cope with?)

There is the cosmetic solution: A swish of twenty-four-hour deodorant or vaginal spray will do wonders to assure you of a night of passionate all-fulfilling love-making.

Sometimes feminine perfection calls only for a can opener and some tomato paste or evaporated milk, and voila, you treat your on-rushing husband to a gourmet feast, followed by an evening of giggling and whispering little nothings.

I have read that commercials are becoming more and more realistic. I understand that they use ordinary looking gals now, just like you and me, to push their products. Well, maybe they are ordinary like you, but they aren't ordinary like me at all.

For one thing, they're all so snappily dressed and coiffured that I'm embarrassed at the inevitable jeans and sweater I tug on every morning. Oh, I have slacks and cute shirts, even a pants suit or two; but I never wear them when I mop the floor. Do you? Yet, those ladies on television scrub the toilet bowl in pantyhose, mini-skirts, and mod shoes. I don't even wear my "good" sneakers when I do the cleaning chores!

By evening, those TV gals are just getting warmed up. Mom has thrown together her own marvelous meat-loaf and serves it with a song. Her children fork every luscious bite into their eager little mouths. Now, in my house, I wearily put together a stew which I dish up in the kitchen to save washing up extra serving platters; the kids slide sulkily down in their seats and try to kill time until dessert—if there is any.

Healthwise, I'm a real failure. All these years my whole family (and I hang my head in shame as I write this) has been using the same bathroom cup. Even worse, I never gave it a second thought until I heard an efficient young mother on a daytime commercial tell me that I am passing colds around. What I should do is use a paper cup dispenser as she does. (I tried it, and my children found countless reasons to use those cups— thanks again to TV—so in twelve minutes, the dispenser was empty.)

Not only that, but I've been buying whatever bandages the local supermarket has on sale, never giving one thought to whether or not they were "ouchless." I have been brutally yanking bandages off my kids' knees when I could have been buying a special brand just for youngsters. That's the kind of mother I am.

If these women don't make you feel guilty enough to buy every new product that hits the shelves, TV has a backup plan—the husband. Husbands are often portrayed as good-natured but blundering slobs, totally dependent upon their wizardlike wives to keep them in sweet-smelling undershirts. All the old man wants is a good meal, a tidy home, a mother-spouse. Look at Rocky Graziano—just a basic guy who loves to eat. So what if he can't express himself like the Galloping Gourmet. Who cares? You know that you're letting him down if you're not responsible enough to buy that special salad dressing for his supper, or serve him the latest high-protein, low-calorie breakfast cereal so he can stay fit. It's the least you can do.

Sometimes the husbands are invisible though still influential, like the one whose wife just found the perfect window cleaner.

"Now I even get corners clean," boasts the first of three utterly demented-looking women.

"No streaks, even in sunshine," drones number two.

"My husband loves how my windows shine," beams the last.

One gets the impression that these ladies have been searching all their lives for this ultimate window cleaner, and now that they've discovered it, their world is complete.

What they have been searching for is acceptance, society's stamp of approval on their immaculate houses, our culture's kiss for their unselfish sacrifice to family happiness—all a part of what we have been led to equate with womanhood.

Women in television commercials are openly portrayed as mindless subservients. If the wives don't tell us this themselves, their husbands do it. One assures us that he will "keep her" because the Mrs. serves on all the right local committees, brushes her hair every night, keeps the house sparkling, and takes a daily iron pill so she can be up to continuing this round of servitude another day. Why shouldn't he keep her?

What television advertisements are drilling into us is the conviction that housework is the grand plan for every "truly feminine" woman, as long as she uses the right product, of course. Ironing with *the* right spray starch is a satisfying experience. Dusting with one certain polish will bring the much-to-be-desired result of neighbors' envious faces. If you buy the wrong brand, you deserve the drudgery it will bring, your family's embarrassment, and your friends' scorn.

We women know how demoralizing it is to watch as those commercials, day in and evening out, beat out their message of predestination for every woman, regardless of her talents, inclinations, yearnings. They strive to convince us that our finest hour is when husband and children praise us for a moist cake and no-ring-around-the-collar white shirts. Our moment of glory comes when a neighbor has to admit that her wash is not as bright as ours, and asks what detergent we use. Is that where our lives, our education, our minds are leading us?

Not long ago Cadwell Davis, an advertising agency, conducted a survey which proved that most American women detest the commercials that portray women in so moronic a way. Franchellie Cadwell, president of the agency, in a speech before her colleagues, attacked "these horrendous commercials, created by men for women, that contemporary women find insulting beyond endurance."

Television has been at this game a long time. In 1963, Betty Friedan wrote in *The Feminine Mystique*:

"The manipulators and their clients in American business can hardly be accused of creating the feminine mystique. But they are the most powerful of its perpetuators; it is their millions which blanket the land with persuasive images, flattering the American housewife, diverting her guilt and disguising her growing sense of emptiness. They have done this so successfully, employing the techniques and concepts of modern social science, and transporting them into those deceptively simple, clever, outrageous ads and commercials, that an observer of the American scene today accepts as fact that the great majority of American women have no ambition other than to be housewives. If they are not solely responsible for sending women home, they are surely responsible for keeping them there. Their unremitting harangue is hard to escape in this day of mass communications; they have seared the feminine mystique deep into every woman's mind, and into the minds of her husband, her children, her neighbors. They have made it part of the fabric of her everyday life, taunting her because she is not a better housewife, does not love her family, is ever growing old."

Commercials have been structured around the concept of what has been termed "the tyranny of 'should.' " We have been raised with, and enveloped in, a cocoon of male-made "shoulds"—we "should" be submissive, we "should" serve our families, we "should" stifle any aggressive traits, and we "should" buy this product because it will prove to everyone that we are truly feminine. The very basis of these commercials, therefore, is erroneous. How can any woman, any human being, live up to that television housewife ideal? It's not even an ideal most of us want to be. What we "should" be, after all, is ourselves.

Womanhood or femininity does not hinge upon serving others. Belonging to the female sex or the male sex entails exactly the same assets and liabilities. Marriage connotes a partnership in life, not slavery, not one-sided supportiveness; wife is not synonymous with geisha, even in Japan. And, our husbands do not treasure us for smooth hands, savory salads, or even (believe it or not) fresh-brewed coffee. They should regard us as people, admirable or not.

In the same vein, being a mother should imply the qualities of leadership and example, rather than the scullery work we have to do in the course of our lives. Will your children remember you for having bought the highest priced margarine or the smoothest peanut butter for your family, or because you washed baby's diapers in the mildest detergent? About the mother who has dedicated herself completely to family, children all too often remark, "Mother slaved hard all her life for us." How brutally direct that is, and how transparently it displays their guilt mixed in with a fat dose of pity. Is that how you want to be remembered?

I don't mean that we housewives should go on strike and from now on refuse to scrub floors, do the dishes, cook meals, or change the baby (tempting as all this may sound). We can't all afford maids, and even if we could, and we carried this idea to its limit, we'd have to hire male maids since all the female maids would be striking too. Someone has to do dull labor. Men have, after all, a great deal of triviality in their work too. The most brilliant lawyer, illustrious scientist, dedicated physician, and even the President of the United States have certain drab chores they must do. Children have school subjects they don't like; housewives have the toilet bowl to scrub.

But let's put the toilet bowl into perspective, shall we? That lawyer, scientist, physician, and President are not rated on the trivialities they perform. Neither should the toilet's sparkling condition mean more than that it is relatively free of germs; let's not be *that* proud to let the bridge club use it. The dust-free furniture should not be our key to successful entertaining, nor should a spot-free water glass equal culinary artistry. All it means is a clean table, clear glass, and sanitary bathroom. Nothing more. Most of all, this clean-complex should not be the basis for a successful life—unless we want it to be, and few women do.

If we have unsavory house chores to do, why can't they be put in second place, after our personally fulfilling work, be it painting, writing, teaching, or other outside employment. Let's cut corners as much as possible. One way to do this is to offer to other members of our families the "joy of participating in the running of a home."

Most important, don't feel guilty about it. If mother is busy doing her thing like everyone else, no one will resent it—once they get used to the idea. Really. Men have accommodated themselves to cooking at the barbecue pit—why not at the kitchen stove as well? Your son can learn that it's just as masculine to flip hamburgers in the house as outside. Daughters can be taught that feigning helplessness before a fusebox is no sure road to whatever is at the end of her rainbow.

Of course, this takes time and determination on your part. A couple we know are well aware of just how much determination is called for. Their teenage daughter and preteen son take turns at the kitchen sink every night after supper.

"Alice is great with the dishes," admits the father, "no problems there. But Tommy tries everything to get out of it. He lets the water run long before any dishes are even in the sink; he washes everything in cold water; grease is all over the drying towels. He even

tells us that he's afraid to be downstairs by himself so
someone has to keep him company. But we persevere.
He must understand that distasteful and time consum-
ing though it may be, the dishes have to be washed,
and there's no reason why he shouldn't take his turn
at them."

As I said—patience and perseverance. The old
cushion of "It's easier to do it myself" has to be thrown
away with the rest of the garbage in a liberated
household.

There are no set rules for every family to follow
because there are degrees of drudgery which vary with
every individual. Like, my mother enjoys ironing while
I sent my shower-gift ironing board down to the base-
ment with the other nonessentials (my husband's tools
are there too, which speaks for his own liberation). I
am a "smoother"; I position myself in front of the
clothes dryer those last few minutes of the cycle, ready
to scoop everything out before the wrinkles set in. I
love the convenience of a dryer; my mother likes to
hang clothes out on the line and sniff their fresh-air
smell when dry.

I enjoy cooking and experimenting with foreign
tastes and recipes. Mother is strictly steak and potatoes;
she explains it with "Your father likes simple food"
(actually that's what she cooks, no matter what he pre-
fers). There are women who take a delight in dusting,
and watching the wood take on a patina after their
years of loving care, while others snap a cloth around
when the in-laws are coming and seldom at any other
time.

Finally, the TV commercials tell us that not only

are we to be paragons of service but sexy paragons as well. That's part of the bargain in marriage. Every woman, rich or poor, five to eighty-five, gets the sex sell. From Twist 'n Turn Barbie to the mouth with "pucker power," TV commercials tell us that to be sensuous is to be successful. Without sex appeal, a little girl won't make friends, a teenager will miss dates, the twenty-year-old will not make the altar, and the forty-year-old will lose her man. Sex is used to sell everything from sweater soap to deodorant. The fastest route from kitchen to bedroom is with a cold-water detergent, a can of soup, or a breakfast cereal. The answer to femininity lies in the latest mouthwash, the toothpaste with whiteners, the bra with criss-cross padding, pantyhose that cling, and support that's firm. Without these, don't hope for happiness. Our TV teacher tells us what to do, and then it's up to us.

As author Shulamith Firestone states, "The ads are creating really weird psychological effects. Women are being led to confuse their sexuality with individuality. What kind of sunglasses or bra they wear, whether they're blonde or brunette, whether there's the right kind of wiggle in their walk, becomes absolutely crucial because their total worth as a human being becomes confused with a surface aspect. The ads are virtually generating erotomania in women."

Although television, of all the media, reaches the greatest number of women, it is not the only one with offensive advertising. Every magazine geared for women—and this includes the teenage books—is pregnant with ads promising "true femininity," by which they mean sex appeal, which will guarantee love. Even those magazines aimed at younger age groups peddle vaginal deodorants, which have now become the latest feminine "necessity." Up to a few years ago, women didn't "realize" that there was such a problem as vaginal odor—today it is an intolerable situation which, luckily for us, advertisers are "solving." How did this happen?

In the mid-sixties, a new product was needed to lift the sagging economy, so manufacturers decided to apply a time-tested formula: Create the anxiety, then the need, and finally, *voilà,* comes the solution. Today, vaginal deodorants have become almost a $50 million business. Incidentally, one preteen version comes in four flavors—what does that say about selling sexuality to little girls?

Youngsters are a big market, and not only for chocolate bars. One brassiere manufacturer estimated several years ago that nine-year-old girls are spending $2 million a year on bras. *Seventeen* and *Ingenue,* leading teen monthlies, peddle how-to-catch-a-man hints along with engagement rings. Girls in the adolescent age bracket are taught diamond-clearly that the main purpose of their existence is to be sexually attractive, and thereupon, they can catch a guy. That is the secret of growing up; once a girl has mastered this, she is mature. As an adult, she can carry it further by proving to her family that she is a better servant than any other woman, and her joyous proof is when other women show envy.

Femininity, however, is the birthright of every person born female. It is not a commodity to be sold over the counter like any household cleanser. Yet, while we can admit the truth in this, it's not easy to stop acting like a grown-up Barbie doll after a lifetime of being told what we must do to attain something we've always owned. We are propagandized into insecurity by those confidential, satisfied models, by the TV children who threaten to abandon us for the neighbor who uses the right cake mix, and by the teenagers who sneer, husbands who stray, and acquaintances who whisper behind snowy gloves—all if we don't buy, buy, buy.

Much of what women in the United States think about themselves is dictated by a fistful of giant companies. How dangerous this is! How degrading to our intelligence and our adult mentality. How unjust it is that so few can dictate a majority's rules and roles. Cadwell Davis, the advertising firm, summed much of this up in the following way:

"At the very least, women deserve recognition as being in full possession of their faculties. . . . We know the rumbles have sounded. The revolution is ready, and one of women's first targets will be moronic, insulting advertising. . . . No force has demeaned women more than advertising."

3

The Tube,
the Screen, and Me

If advertising is Number One in projecting an insulting image, the entertainment media must be second. And like all Number Twos, it is running hard to catch up.

Television is the male's "Green Pastures." For the female, it is "The Waste Land." Since the birth of the boob tube, women have been planted in one of three arenas, and each arena holds a stereotype.

As Robin Morgan wrote: "The image of women . . . is dreadful. At one pole there is the 'I Love Lucy' stereotype, the brainless featherhead, and the sweet, dumb lovable blonde of 'Petticoat Junction' and

'Green Acres' who's helpless without men. In between there's the maternal nurturing housewife like Donna Reed or 'Julia'—passive women who are defined in terms of their relationship to men—as wives or mothers or widows. At the other pole there's the male fantasy of the 'liberated' woman—the chic, hard, cold, sexy swinger with no ties, who obviously sleeps around and is not an economic drag on the men. And there's nothing else. It has almost no relationship with reality at all."

Growing up in the fifties was growing up with "I Love Lucy." (So was growing up in the sixties and, obviously, will be in the seventies, as well.) I used to wonder what made Ricky love Lucy at all, much less live with her through such pandemonium and strife. Lucy and Ethel were not even supportive to their men; they were detriments. "Lucy" and her offspring, "That Girl" and "Funny Face," needed men to bail them out of the unbelievable predicaments they found themselves in. They almost justified the concept held by many men that women are sex pets who clean the house but can't do much else. Promise them the latest sewing machine and they'll follow you anywhere. It worked in the fifties—it works today.

Why the success? Because unfortunately we girls believe the myth that women are really not much more than playful kittens (or bunnies). Otherwise, would we have laughed Lucy to her phenomenal stardom? The question is, why do Lucy-Ann Marie-Sandy-ad nauseum get into so much trouble? Mainly frustration. Woman is bored and/or inept; woman searches for excitement; woman gets into trouble; and responsible man rescues her. Result—a comedy. Lucy tries to escape the boredom of being a housewife by breaking into the glamor of show-business. By watching her, other women can fantasize and "escape" as well, and not even get a hint of a scolding from their husbands. Lucy takes it on the chin for all women.

In the second arena, TV has stitched females into a needlepoint of eternal maternity. This is a grand old tradition stretching back to "I Remember Mama." More recent ideals have included a nurse called "Julia," an assistant named Doris Day, a combination assistant-nurse on "Marcus Welby, M.D.," and the old-faithful mother on "My Three Sons." Mom reaches her greatest heights as Jenny on the "New Dick Van Dyke Show." It has been misleading for the credits to label her as Dick's wife; for all practical purposes, Jenny represents his mother just as much as she is the mother of his three children. Better yet, she's Dick's keeper, for without Jenny's tender loving care, Dick would have killed himself in the first episode.

No matter what outside work these women may be doing in their TV worlds, it's maternally geared. Julia went to work only when she had to support her son; ditto Doris. Take Mary Tyler Moore, over-thirty and a noble contender for the "typical single career girl" award; although she loves her job, both feet are pointed toward marriage, not personal advancement.

When we watch these shows year after year, we deduce that a true woman is either a wife, a widow, or a mother. We learn that her first goal must be "femininity." Feminine work is in the home. If there is no home just now, an outside job will keep us in dry cereal and the latest styles, but only until Mr. Right happens along. And meanwhile, who watches all this but our children, and slowly their minds adjust to the same values. Son expects to marry a budding Shirley Partridge; daughter watches her future settle supportively before her, original aims relaxing into nurse, assistant, mother—instead of doctor, editor, bachelor-girl.

This hit home last year when, in a Sunday School questionnaire, my seven-year-old daughter was asked "Who is the happiest person you know?"

"My Aunt Marilyn," responded Jeannine, "because she just got a boyfriend."

Aunt Marilyn is not in such desperate straits that she needs Jeannine's concern. But what bothered me, her feminist mother, was that she was equating happiness with boyfriend. In my despair, I blamed it all on "The Brady Bunch."

It's not that "The Brady Bunch" is a destructive show. There's no slaughter, no bedroom sex, just good wholesome family fun. But for a paranoid role-raker like me, it's a shockingly sexist show.

Sexist, of course, has nothing to do with sexy. "Sexy" is the quality of appealing to the opposite sex. "Sexist" assigns females one entire set of characteristics and males another—and never the twain shall mix. So it is on "The Brady Bunch." And since the Brady daughters are all girly-girly, just as the Brady guys are all, well, guys, it stands to reason that boyfriends must enter the lives of the Brady gals.

Understandable. But I must put my liberated foot down when searching out boyfriends becomes Priority

Number One for the under-eleven set, a problem spelled out very clearly in the episode where the Bunch comes unglued at the thought of their little girl being without (gulp) sex appeal.

That was the show when little Jan returned home from school to answer Mama Brady's solicitous queries, "Did you see him today? What did he say? How did he act?"

And don't put this down as just some feminine man-trapping instinct. Dad Brady was no better. "Did he carry Jan's books home from school?" was his first concern upon returning home from the office. And the answer to that set the mood for the entire evening. If it had been *yes,* all would have been well with the Brady Bunch. But with a *no,* the group attempted to find out why. *What,* they wondered, *is wrong with Jan?*

What was wrong, we learned twenty wretched minutes later, was that Jan did not dress like a girl (and doesn't this all fall "femininely" into place?). She was a tomboy, and we all know that boys don't make passes at girls who wear blue jeans (unless they're much older). What they make passes at are walking, talking Dawn dolls.

You're right, I'm exaggerating. But not too much. What one realizes about shows like "The Brady Bunch," and before that, "Make Room for Daddy" and "Grand-Daddy," and "Bachelor Father," is that the little girls watching would have to be papier-mâché not to learn that snagging a beau is Number One, and schoolwork, intelligence, talent, and girl friends fall to a second spot far behind the boyfriend.

Naturally, we've all gone through a lot of this in

our own growing-up years, with the result that our shrinking world is needlessly sloughing off competent female scientists, physicians, musicians, and so on. At the risk of simplifying a complex problem, television is now as much a part of most families as is one of the children, and when youngsters rack up some fifty-four tube hours a week, it's obvious the grand impact television has on their attitudes. It has certainly influenced their mothers.

The opposite end of this unsavory spectrum is the avenue of adventure shows—adventure for the man, adornment for the woman. If the show's hero is a free-swinger, his mates swing free as well, the products of our so-called "sexual revolution." "The Immortal," "The Fugitive," and the other TV unreals have used equally unreal gals to satisfy their very real needs. Sometimes, as in "Hawaii Five-O," women are hardly involved, except as witnesses or victims. Other times, as in "Mannix," they are prominently cast in secondary roles, answering the phone and worrying about the boss' safety while he does the creative planning and exciting maneuvering.

"Mannix," a spin-off from a long line of who-dunits, used the tried and true formula—vigorous, brilliant detective (male) and dedicated, beautiful help-mate (female). Remember the old "Thin Man" series? Mrs. Thin Man was supposedly an equal partner in their detective activities, yet the Thin *Man* formulated the moves, told his goodwife what to do and where to go, and eventually solved the problem. On "Mannix," the girl Friday is a widow, working—you guessed it— to support her little boy. If she had the chance to get married, it's crystal clear that she would quit in a flash to settle at home, forevermore to flutter around her suburban split-level just as she fluttered around her city office.

Are all these images untrue? Sad to say, no: they are quite valid images because most women are channeled exactly into these slots—housewife or housewife-preparation. Television, movies, and magazines reflect as well as perpetuate the society they are geared for, degrading as it may seem. Women are not typically in positions of power, and so, an unmarried strong female on television is usually portrayed as evil or supernatural—a "Jeannie," the genie. TV tells us very candidly that believable, likeable women are strong in the married sphere, or else they exist only in fantasy.

Yet, if "most" women are found in the domestic line, there should be room made for the exceptions. As long as television will not acknowledge that women physicians exist in most medical centers, and that there are female editors, professors, and business people, and as long as TV will not recognize the potential in all women, it perpetuates a vicious circle. Women are set up as second-raters; our daughters emulate these models and our sons expect someone like them for their future mates. Little girls grow up to fit into these secondary slots and the cycle begins again—like the wheel of a cotton-candy machine turning around and around, spinning a puff of sweet cotton candy which makes you sick when you eat too much of it.

Finally, in regard to television, women have been nudged out of the newsroom, except for the specified "female" areas of fashion shows and civic center cooking demonstrations. And even this much of a toe-in-the-door is relatively recent. Women can cover art, unless it's a Picasso showing, or a society happening if there are no political overtones. In local television, women have been appearing on daytime or late-late-night news broadcasts, but even this is dangerously radical, and the girls are steered toward human-interest rather than current news.

The exception, of course, is Barbara Walters, who gets an occasional whack at a male-oriented interview, although a lot of her time involves chatting with Yves Montand, James Beard, or Ethel Kennedy about films, cooking, or the Kennedy kids.

Actually, many feminists categorize Ms. Walters as a "woman's woman," whose job it is to interpret business and other heavy (male) affairs to women. Yet, women like Barbara, it seems to me, are revealing that females can be as intelligent and witty as men, and very often, more so. She is a far better interviewer than most of the prime-time talkfest hosts, though she occasionally lapses into gushiness. (But I sense that this is a purposeful velvet-glove concession to the female image.) And she is moving onward—in June 1971, she was predictably assigned to cover the Nixon-Cox nuptials, but eight months later she scooped many male colleagues by traveling to China with the President.

Barbara interprets "men's affairs" to women, but most other female talk stars interpret "women's affairs" to women. Hopefully, there will be a redefining of "women's affairs" to include economy, ecology, education, health, and politics, as well as that faithful standby, cooking. Women like Bess Myerson and Betty

Furness are articulate in discussing these human issues. However, most women TV stars are still maneuvered into Dinah Shore-type sewing hints, Betsy Palmer-type girl-talk, and Virginia Graham-type gossip sessions by men who discovered a gap in the TV roster and decided this void would be most profitably filled by feminine flummery. Yet, if Graham Kerr can cook and get away with it gorgeously, why can't Dinah get into something more intoxicating than the new hem lengths?

The "female image" in Hollywood is like a punctured balloon figure—the body is there but not the form. Like television, the movies portray women in one dimension—parental or pornographic. Whereas TV emphasizes the former, films of the seventies stress the porno view of women. While the male characters are straining to buck the System, their women are straining just to exist. Women in contemporary films are either mindless mounds of flesh or, if they are portrayed as mentally alive at all, they are concentrating on destroying their men. (Even this destructiveness is considered to be innate: Portnoy's mother stifles her son just by being a mother; in "Five Easy Pieces," the waitress drives Bobby, our "hero," up the wall simply by being a dumb broad.)

Women in films seem to have no control of their own lives. There, in living color, women are symbols of a perverted version of the female sex. They represent all the clichés ever used *against* women—passive, castrating, gentle, conniving, and nympho or frigid.

Except for one brief period during the Depression years, this is pretty much the way women have always been represented by the Celluloid masters. What is interesting to note is that actresses become sex symbols, yet actors project sex appeal. And, yes, there is a difference between the two.

Leon Salzman, M.D., a professor of psychiatry, once defined sex appeal in *Medical Aspects of Human Sexuality* as incorporating "the notion of enduring sexual interest and a continuing impetus for greater involvement." It offers not just a one-night infatuation but a lingering affair (or the promise of one). A person with sex appeal has charisma—something more than the cling of one's clothes or the line of one's body. It is what Dr. Salzman calls "the variety of characteristics . . . which act directly as an erotic stimulation." And since it involves more than just the physical, others of the same sex can appreciate it. Think how many male fans Clark Gable and Paul Newman have.

However, a sex symbol is only a wedge of the total pie of sex appeal. A sex symbol has been described as an animated version of the *Playboy* centerfold, a doll, an exterior which is empty inside. In fact, many acknowledged sex symbols have gotten their first exposure in the girlie publications.

Why has this happened to women? Why does a sexy man embody sex appeal while a sexy woman is a cardboard object? Perhaps because ever since the age of mass sex began, just after World War I, movies have been written, produced, directed, and photographed by men. From the start, male actors were given roles with gumption, excitement, dimension. Roles and actors have changed with the times: dashing and romantic in the twenties; threateningly glamorous in the thirties; hale and hearty during the war years; and searchingly sensitive today.

Women did not have that challenge. The only time in movie history that women rose above the bosom sex level was in the thirties, a heyday for good gutsy female sex stars. Not objects, mind you, for actresses like Constance Bennett and Joan Crawford were landing parts they could sink their teeth into, parts with personality, character, and passion. Joan Blondell and Carole Lombard talked racy and acted sharp. Men adored them, and women admired them. They were sexy and anything but empty.

Most of these movie characters turned out to be good-hearted dames who were being slung about by Life. Rough treatment was the rule on how to handle them. Tallulah Bankhead, Barbara Stanwyck, Marlene Dietrich, and Greta Garbo all had good reasons for taking up with the likes of Cagney, Gable, and Robinson—something like having a kid sister to put through school or a baby to feed. It wasn't empty sex motivating them, but a purer reason which every tenement dweller, male and female, in Depression America could sympathize with.

But, for women, that was the brief Golden Age. In the forties, the curtain closed, and the Plastic Age was upon us. Men were leaving to fight a patriotic war and, to spur them on, they dreamed of voluptuous Betty Grable and Dorothy Lamour. Another young lady in a sweater propelled a whole new standard of female beauty; Lana Turner turned the country away from the crepe-y look of the thirties to the well-mounded breast as the new banner of sex. Other glamor girls followed, and often lived tragic lives as they searched for the real Rita Hayworth or Ava Gardner beneath that sexy surface. The more turbulent and scandalous their lives became, the more voracious grew their fans, always demanding more publicity. And always getting it.

Notoriety, however, was only for sex objects. When a qualified actress like Ingrid Bergman dared to slap morality in the face and bear a child out of wedlock, the country roared in outrage. In 1950, the senior senator from Colorado castigated her as a "powerful influence for evil." Ingrid was sexy, but she was an actress as well. Her audience decided that only objects had the right to sin, so she was banished.

With the peace and prosperity of the fifties came also conformity, especially in the case of sex idols. They were as American as apple pie and Joe McCarthy. Bland and blonde Marilyn Monroe bloomed forth as the sex object of all time. She was as feminine as the back-to-the-home movement; the eternal female every other American woman was to imitate. She was helpless and human, soft and submissive. The only problem was that Marilyn tried to break out of the trap. Although society sympathized with her attempts to become a good actress, her image was stamped too deep, and finally, she was destroyed.

The 1950s was an era when masculinity and femininity were "in" and male-female roles were not to be tampered with. Rock Hudson, Tab Hunter, and Robert Wagner were the "nice" boys, but they didn't break any stereotypes, any more than James Dean or Marlon Brando ("bad" boys) did. And during this decade

erupted the phenomenon that made women the cari-
catures they are today—*Playboy* magazine. And isn't
that just what most of the readers are? Boys, "playing"
at being men?

The buyers of *Playboy* can ogle and fantasize, but
hands off! Unlike earlier girlie books, *Playboy* can be
purchased openly from the newsstand. The boys can
play at being intellectuals too, for many articles are
admittedly worthwhile. But we all know what the real
draw is, and interviews with Galbraith or Rod McKuen
have nothing to do with it.

If a man likes to look at nubile nudies, that's fine.
But *Playboy* goes one step further. It sells sex advice as
well as the magazine, and peddles nighties, undies,
and how-to's along with the club key. It suggests which
stereo records will do the most for the swinger's circular bed with satin sheets, and which cosmetics are
machismo. And all for what? Why, it's flypaper for the
fly, or Bunny, a cuddly, padded, cinched-in Bunny, all
wriggling and ready to titillate.

Gloria Steinem prefaced her interview with Hugh
Hefner in *McCalls* with: "Buy all these things, plus,
of course, *Playboy*, at a dollar a throw, for instructions
on how to use them, and what can possibly go wrong?
Because women are objects too; objects whose only
peculiar property is an attraction to other objects, so
that they will arrive on the scene automatically, like a
prize for collected Green Stamps, after the proper
string of purchases has been made."

The film (and hard-cover book) version of the
Playboy idea was the James Bond of the sixties, who
put the finishing touches on Female Mechanization.

His women were nothing more than sexual robots, devoid of individuality. In a decade when Ringo Starr, Woody Allen, and Dustin Hoffman seemed sexy to women, the "ideal" woman was Raquel Welch, another in the long line of Hayworths and Mansfields. And female roles included sex-crazed Mrs. Robinson, freaky Myra Breckenridge, and later, the frustrated war-nurses of *M*A*S*H*.

Women are still locked behind the plastic door, although a few former sex symbols have begun to demand a new image. Jane Fonda is one example, although many put her down as "just a woman" who is satisfying her ego and capitalizing on her fame by protesting for any cause in sight. In an article for the *New York Times,* she wrote, "Men see me coming and they say, 'Ecch, bring me back the old-time movie star. We want a body and a face, we don't want this uppity woman.' . . . This is what we have to begin to change."

Serious actresses who happen to be physically well-endowed usually have a long, unfair battle if they want to get out of this tight-drawn bag. For every human Jeanne Moreau, there are three vacant Jill St. Johns. For every Katherine Houghton (who refused movie roles for several years after *Guess Who's Coming To Dinner* because she felt the attitude toward women was cruel and inhumane), there is an Ann-Margret ready to capitalize.

This is not to discount beauty. However, beauty is *part* of a whole person; it is not a substitute for a person. It can work *for* a woman: Sophia Loren is more of an actress and a human being now than she was fifteen years ago. Gina Lollobrigida, on the other hand, is impassioned only in her fight against aging.

Is it so unreal to portray women on the screen with depth, mystery, and excitement? Women whose charisma can endure as male stars' have? Of course, it is up to the American woman herself to believe that female sex appeal is an inner passion and attitude rather than an outer convexity.

Myths which took centuries to build up are hard to shatter; however, the cracks are already etched across the walls.

4

Growing Up
With Mother

I know how fashionable it has been to blame all
of life's ills on mother, whether she be Jewish, Catholic,
Black, Wasp, or other. I have no intention here of producing any kind of maternal hate-sheet (far be it from
me, a feminist mother of two, to downgrade my accomplishments in the arena of bringing up baby). In addition, I feel it is only fair to acknowledge the other half's
role in daughter raising.

Psychologists agree that it is the father of the family who writes the rules on masculinity and femininity.
Father is usually the first man in a girl's life and his
attitude toward her goes far in determining how she

will eventually regard men in adulthood. If he chooses to raise his daughter much as he does his son, both have a better chance of growing up equally self-sufficient. What usually happens, however, is that fathers like to see their kids acting like miniature adults; they demand that their sons be little men, and not cry or whimper, and their daughters be huggable little ladies.

It is up to mother to see that the children set out on the right paths toward femininity and masculinity. Usually, mom is inclined to give fairly equal treatment to young sons and daughters; she disciplines whoever is naughty without too much regard for whether the offender is male or female—at least in the early years. We cuddle our little boys as much as our girls, and empathize with masculine bruises as compassionately as with feminine bruises.

However, mothers do want daughters and sons to be acceptable to others in life, and acceptability often strolls hand in hand with conformity. Since life for a woman is still primarily dependent upon the men in her life, mother finds herself following the rules written by her husband, and she proceeds to set the roles for kiddies to follow.

What is phenomenal is how quickly children learn these roles. Just compare the following two kids and see how each sex has learned the most effective way to approach father for a favor.

Junior usually strides right up, takes a stand, and makes his point. "Dad," he begins, "I need a new baseball mitt."

"What's the matter with the one you have?"

"It's too old and it's ripping."

Boys are encouraged to speak out, not whine or lallygag. Step right up and spit it out.

Sister, now, is another matter. She usually takes the old sideways approach. My own daughter, Jeannine, tried this technique at seven. She had a girl friend visiting and decided that it would be fun for daddy to drive them out somewhere for ice cream. However, this would take some doing because it was so close to dinner time. So, when Jeannine heard her father drive up after work and open the front door, she cried out to her friend in a booming voice: "Boy, Debbie, wait till you meet my dad! He's tall with lots of hair and he's so much fun. Maybe he'll throw us in the air and take us out for ice cream!"

My husband would have had to be deaf not to hear. The "lots of hair" part was probably pretty tempting, but daddy is wise in the ways of little girls and their suppers, so no ice cream. He did, however, make Jeannine's effort worthwhile by giving her some chewing gum he had brought home. Whether or not that was an adequate substitute for ice cream, I can't say; all I do know is that it provided Jeannine with some reward for her performance, enough to encourage her to try it again.

I use the word *performance,* but performing does not necessarily imply insincerity. Little girls are encouraged from pink-blanket days to employ devious means of getting around men. "Acting" feminine becomes as natural as eating and sleeping, and it is a lesson learned as thoroughly as any schoolwork, and much faster. Do things dad's way, and you'll get what you want. More important, he'll love you for it.

If you will allow me to digress right now, I'd like to introduce you to Emily, a kindly old lady who always proffers the highest compliments to our children, though I must admit that she does the same for most children. Emily is one of those rare human beings who not only likes but enjoys children—all ages and sizes. However, her "high compliments" tend to run in parallels—one line is feminine, the other masculine.

"Oh," she coos at our Jason, "he's all boy."

"And Jeannine," turning to our daughter, "a real little lady."

We all know that boys and girls come into the world in identical fashion, but from cord-cutting on, one takes the high road, the other the low. Or, to put it another way, boys become rough, tough "snakes and snails, and puppy-dog tails," while girls turn into "sugar and spice, and everything nice."

Now that doesn't sound so bad, does it? But if we dissect the problem a little more, we discover that "sugar and spice, and everything nice" is rather limiting. It's mixed up with baking and smiles and gentle beguiles, tucked in tissue paper, snuggled in a cardboard box, and tied with a fluff of pink ribbon. And there it sits, hoping a Prince Charming will claim it before the box gets dusty and the ribbon limp.

When child-loving Emily nods at Jason's all boyness, she is really condoning his aggressive activity, his muscle building, tree climbing, and bang-bang-I'm-preparing-myself-for-the-cruel-world attitude. When she smiles at Jeannine's "little lady" behavior, she acknowledges that, for a girl, preparing-for-the-cruel-world means acting benign and dependent, and applauding while someone else (a male) does the building and the tree scaling.

Naturally, we all know children don't fit exactly into these roles, anymore than women and men fit into their ultimate extensions. Just as a father may be a poetic dreamer, a son may be most contented when curled up in the corner of the sofa reading a book. And mother may be Mrs. Executive, while daughter pitches for the neighborhood Little League (if such an integrated Little League actually exists). But these are the rebels, the individualists, the unique—they are not the ideals. And when we bring up our children, we steer straight for the ideals, which Emily classifies as "all boy" and "little lady."

Like other women, Emily received her ideals from men. Women have traditionally battled and bickered among themselves for the grand prize, a husband. So naturally they long ago adopted the qualities most men wanted in a woman. Mothers instill them in their daughters. Since dad wants "femininity," well, it's mother's job to set daughter on the right road, gathering up appropriate accoutrements on the way, like clothing, hairdos, and the most effective of all old faithfuls—charm.

There is precious little variation allowed here; for boys, virtually none. They are not allowed to rebel by donning feminine clothes nor by playing with dolls (except G.I. Joe); teachers become uneasy when little boys hang around the nursery school's kitchen corner instead of the truck corner. Little girls who rebel are tolerated as tomboys but only in a very limited sense. It is made clear that boyish behavior is undesirable.

When daughter gets older she will adjust and become just as much a lady as Nanette down the street. In fact, when the day comes that daughter finally relents and mimics little Nanette, she is rewarded, perhaps with a designer party dress and a permanent wave. It doesn't take much to convince kids that it pays to play the game.

In short, growing up with mother means, first of all, growing up to be a lady. In the dictionary, *lady* means a woman in a socially prominent position, and isn't this what every mother wants for her darling daughter? And what's the best way to reach this pinnacle? Marriage, of course. And how does one catch an eligible passport to prestige? By acting feminine, and demonstrating "maternal instinct" (a catch-all phrase that we'll get to later). And who is better equipped to teach feminine behavior than mama? Even if she may have married someone less than a lord, she still has her visions, and no one is more available to fulfill those long-ago dreams than her own little lady-in-the-bud.

Some mothers vary in their aims. There are those who desire wealth and position for their little girls; others just want a good man. Some feel education and culture will net a fine husband; others vaguely push for "a better life than I had." But all mothers agree on one point—they want their daughters to be happy, and traditionally happiness is a husband and family. And for this, you have to be a lady.

Mother teaches us very early that the most exciting and satisfying career for a woman is marriage to a great man. But if you can't get a great man (after all, there aren't that many around, even for extraordinary daughters), most any man will do. Mothers soon get down to the nitty-gritty, practical side of life, which is survival, and for a woman to survive, she must learn the cultural network of "femininity." This they begin teaching immediately, from the day the pink bundle comes home.

Babies look pretty neutral at the start, at least with diapers on, so it is up to mother to make sure nobody misinterprets what's in the bundle. She does this by dressing baby girls in pink and boys in blue.

Step two is dressing up baby girls in all the frills mother can get her hands on, perhaps sensing that it won't be long before frills and fluff aren't practical anymore for crawling, dirt-eating two-year-olds of either sex. Granted, there are cute clothes for baby boys, but it's just not as much fun dressing them up because it's not really as important for a little boy to be handsomely turned out. Boys are appealing as they dart around, messing, grabbing, or slapping spoons against pots. Baby girls, now, we enjoy seeing clean and adorable, like stuffed dolls.

Dressing up daughter can compensate for that future time when we will discourage her from activity and competition. It is one way of enjoying the new baby, too, especially if mother originally wanted a boy (not only for herself, but to satisfy husband, in-laws, or parents).

My friend Jane never discussed the possibility that the child she was carrying might, just *might,* turn out to be a girl.

"It's a boy and we're naming him Brett," she insisted.

Of course, she gave birth to a baby girl.

Jane was undaunted (women are great accommodators). "We're still naming her Brett, after the heroine in *The Sun Also Rises.*"

And Jane proceeded to maneuver Brett into all those starched lilliputian dresses she had received as gifts. However, there weren't that many chances for dressing baby up, since even baby girls tend to spit up on everything, and it wasn't worth washing, starching, and pressing those minuscule things when they might not even make it out of the house.

In addition, Jane doggedly pinned teeny bows in little Brett's rather impressive head of black hair. She would have progressed to satin ribbons but at that point Brett developed an unfortunate case of cradle cap and her hair had to be shorn. (It's only fair to add that this affliction had nothing at all to do with pinning bows in a two-month-old infant's hair.)

Boys get the same sexist treatment. When Martha had her second child (first boy), the proud father welcomed his new son home from the hospital to a crib filled with tiny baseballs, footballs, basketballs, catcher's mitts, bats, a helmet, hockey pucks, and so on.

This would not be too unexpected if this father were some famous Saturday afternoon sports hero— but he isn't even a Saturday afternoon sports fan. Mark has a doctorate in literature, writes poetry, and dabbles in acrylic painting; yet, he is determined that his son will get a firm push in the accepted direction. Mark himself might never spend his days playing catch with junior, but no one can accuse him of not providing the correct equipment.

Speaking of cribs—have you noticed the rooms we decorate for sons and daughters? A boy's room must yell "masculine!" For an infant son, we might try for a light, happy atmosphere, conducive of breezy activity—a bright circus motif or sailboats. When he gets older we switch to the American Revolution or racing car themes. The main idea is to give him a room to jump, climb, and romp in, with trucks, trailers, speedboats, and baseball bats in abundance, and perhaps a hatrack to inspire him in his games of fireman, Indian, cowboy, and astronaut.

The decor is sturdy and functional; even son's curtains are permapress, subdued, and straight. In fact, the whole room is an area for a child to experiment, create, and grow in, but it's not a room in which to snuggle into a soft chair and read.

Turn next to a typical bedroom for a little girl. Frilly dotted-swiss curtains on the windows, a starched organdy bedspread with dust ruffle, perhaps a four-poster to keep her even more contained. A room that says "Don't touch and keep neat." She may have a bookshelf with reading material set in a tidy row (little girls are encouraged to *read* rather than *do*). And finally, all around is displayed her collection of dolls, "Talking Drowsy," "Busy Betsy," Raggedy Ann, and Barbie, and the not-to-be-touched collection of costumed dolls from around the world (probably belonging more to mother than to daughter). We push dolls on little girls as if we'd better get that motherhood role drilled in before they develop any other ideas.

In fact, I think mothers often get more involved with these dolls than the children do. One of my best friends reacted strongly when her daughter left a favorite doll in the playground. In a frenzy, Betsy, the mother, called me up. "You live near the park," she cried. "Would you please run over and see if you can find 'Dollie'? Kathy will never go to sleep without that doll. She's had it since she was born."

Sure, I'd try. And off I went to search the wastepaper baskets, swings, sandboxes, the grass, the benches —but no "Dollie."

Betsy was almost in tears when I called to tell her. She was worried about how her little girl would face life without the beloved "Dollie."

"It was Kathy's first present," Betsy wailed.

"Has she been crying?" I asked.

"No. In fact, Kathy doesn't seem to miss 'Dollie' at all. I'm sure she doesn't realize that the doll is actually gone."

Well, folks, "Dollie" was never found, and the most Kathy did was ask rather placidly about her doll when she was ready for bed that night. Betsy gently told her that she'd have to sleep with the other dolls that night, and they'd look for "Dollie" again in the morning. Kathy promptly fell asleep, and "Dollie" was forgotten. But not by mother. It took several days for Betsy to calm down and resign herself to having lost a sentimental relic of her daughter's infancy.

Many mothers buy dolls as much for themselves as for their children. Watching a little girl fuss over her doll seems proof that she is well along the sexist road. So well along, in fact, that mothers next begin presenting daughters with the accompaniments for doll-fussing.

Big mothers, it seems, are particularly generous about buying the little-mother category of toys, because these prepare little girls for ladyhood, which is that ineluctable first step to wifehood. In the tapestry of a woman's life, motherhood forms the distinctive pattern. Arts, crafts, sports, and hobbies have their places, but they're second places; it's better to train for housework first. What the mother is telling the daughter is "Get the husband, then you can have your hobbies."

"Laurie is bothering the life out of me for that Quick-Bake oven," a neighbor complained to me last Christmas. Then she smiled and sighed, "They want everything they see on TV, don't they?"

Sure they do. So would you if you had a good chance of getting it. The limits we set and the lines we draw depend on us, and obviously, little-mother accessories are fine with most practicing big mothers. Children are rather indiscriminate about wanting. They want everything, the more the merrier. And I'm sure every mother puts some boundaries on what she allows her children to get from among the items offered by the television salespitch, whether that line be drawn at sexual objects, such as grown-up dolls with their curvy bikini-ed bodies or toy machine guns to teach the joy of killing.

In this training ground for adulthood, little girls are being prepared for half a life, and so are their brothers. She is headed straight for domesticity; he is headed for a "meaningful career." Both are sent in parallel and separate-but-unequal paths to adulthood. Somewhere, individuality has been trampled down, unless it applies to sexist aims. And once again, brother has the better road, because he has options—engineering, medicine, and so on—and her choice is one. To want anything other than a baby is abnormal.

"But children need direction," you may say.

I agree. But have you noticed that when we supply little boys with those trucks, planes, and cowboy boots, we are not telling them that they are to eventually grow up to become truck drivers, pilots, or ranchers? We give them a range of choices, a chance to experiment on various training grounds. When we drown our daughters in doll carriages and "Shoppin' Sheryls," we are telling them that domesticity is what they should aim for. Compare the wide variety of toys available for boys to the few types of domestic toys for girls.

Not only is daughter bombarded with house-toys, she is also sold the sexual image of Barbie or Dawn. And there is a new version every year, with a handy line of material accompaniments so you can be relieved of the decision of what to get daughter next birthday. What Barbie-type dolls sell is a fantasy that centers around the opposite sex, a style of swinging, teen worship, and rejection of all other aspects of society and of contributing to them. Daughter will grow up to desire the cars and campers that Barbie has, and to believe that this material will help her to lure her own personal Ken. Ken is where Barbie's aims end; Barbie is the supreme sex object.

We use very few criteria in raising children other than sex, especially in the early and most absorbent years. Our little boys get no preparation at all for marriage and fatherhood. We convince girls that eventually these cantankerous little rascals called "boys" will change their minds and "accept" girls to be their mates. We clamp our daughters into subordinate molds almost before they can walk.

Children, it is believed, reach the half-way mark in intelligence by the time they are four years old. By that time, little girls have their stuffed animals, starched-curtained rooms, their dolls, their Quick-Bake ovens. They iron with mother, peel potatoes, and set the table. Once in a while, daddy may take them to the circus or zoo, all dressed up in a new ruffled dress, straw hat, and clutching a patent leather handbag, and remembering the admonition, "Act like a lady. Don't get dirty." And, as an afterthought, and least important of all, "Oh, yes, and have a good time, dear."

Certainly we teach girls the three Rs, send them to the same schools, and expose them to the same teachers as we do the boys. But what do the girls reap from schoolbooks? More of the same.

Early in the seventies, a group of mothers, teachers, psychologists, students, and businesswomen from Princeton, New Jersey, delved into some of the textbooks children were reading. The study took almost a year and reached into 144 of the most widely used school texts from primer to sixth grade, including those from twelve of the major textbook publishers.

What did they find? "Approximately seventy-two percent of the stories about individual children were geared to forty-nine percent of the young reading population." That is, the boys.

Even more significant was the quality of the stories. The study concluded that school readers are "a powerful influence in stunting a girl's growth." They are drilling into her "the subliminal message that she is an inferior, secondary person." How? By a distorted portrayal of little girls and their mothers. Today, when schools are supposed to be soul-searching in the attempt to improve, textbooks are back in the Stone Age, at least from the little girls' point of view. The basis of girl-boy "roles" has nothing to do with intelligence, character, personality, or physical prowess — only gender.

Girls are pictured as spectators of life, watching as the boys excel. Males are stronger, older, more capable, while the girls are frightened and passive. Boys expand their horizons beyond the home, but if a little girl ventures out, it is to buy eggs for her mother. Her link with the outside world is her very own telephone call. Can you blame boys for scowling "She's only a girl!" when this sort of bias is right in their schoolbooks?

Mother is just a tall version of daughter. She is drawn with no outside activities, and even in the home, she stands in the background, coming forth only to offer her newest batch of cookies. Problems are for dad to solve. Even the male-female faces are sketched differently: mother's is vapid and blank, while dad's face is animated.

The textbooks tell your daughter that if she is curious and active, she is abnormal. This is a distortion, for little girls outdo boys all through grade school, and their mothers, rather than staying in the house, are very likely to be out working.

Television works the same way. Recently, I began an informal study of sexism in children's television shows, so I asked my daughter, who was watching TV, to tell me whenever a woman was featured.

"I found one!" she cried while watching "Mr. Rogers' Neighborhood." She was jubilant because there just aren't that many women on children's shows.

"What is she doing?" I called.

"She's a servant," Jeannine replied. "She's cleaning the castle."

Hmmm. Enough said. Combined with textbooks, television starts the girl well on her road over the rainbow to where the big pot of gold—femininity—sits waiting for her. "Captain Kangaroo," "Sesame Street," and "Electric Company" are all pretty much male-run businesses. And as for the action cartoons, they provide plenty of fantasy material for little boys, but where is a daredevil lady for the little girl to identify with?

There are, of course, fairy tales for her fantasies—Rapunzel, Snow White, Cinderella, Sleeping Beauty. Here little girls learn fast that everyone loves the lovelies, especially those with alluring passivity, lying around waiting for Love (the Prince) to fulfill their destinies. What we have to watch out for are the old crones, because girls understand early that once they get old, they automatically turn into evil witches. Not old men, though. They're kindly Captain Kangaroos.

Finally, daughters learn that women have something called "maternal instinct." This myth tells of a feminine inborn trait which includes serving and dedicating oneself to the family and to society, as well as an instinctive love for offspring. Mothers are innately supposed to know how to do things for others, like bake cookies, change diapers, and do the laundry.

Women have all this within them and their job is to show their daughters how to bring out their "maternal instinct" as well, as though it were a grand tradition. Mothers are like a kind of animated wind-up doll which makes sure kids get hot breakfasts and wear clean underwear; they whisk around their houses like devoted ghosts, snatching lint from carpets and grease stains from kitchen walls, creating wombs outside the womb where the gang can always come home to roost before emerging into the world again. And if a mother is not up to the standards of television and storybooks, daughter, at some point of her development, declares piously, "I'm going to be different from her. I'll be a good mother."

From all this, boys learn something too. They surmise that girls are pretty inferior characters, not strong, afraid of bugs, disliking challenges. But boys know that all girls grow up, and that's when they start coming in handy. That's when they become wives and mothers, keeping the house going and the cookies coming while the guys keep the world going and the money coming. Like daddy does.

Perhaps the greatest detriment comes from ourselves, in the form of the ultimate threat directed at a child at that time, usually in the late afternoon when we are preparing supper, setting the table, straightening the living room, and turning down the TV volume. We slap on a dash of lipstick and suddenly our youngest bursts in demanding a peanut butter sandwich.

"No," we say.

"I want one!" he yells, ill with five o'clock crankiness. "I'm hungry."

"It's almost dinner time," we rasp, trying to keep calm. It won't be much longer, we tell ourselves, a vulnerable time of day, keep going kid . . .

But our youngest does not understand that we are getting together a cream sauce, hopefully without lumps, that our day has been one of minor but mounting trials, and that the whine of a four-year-old can scrape across our nerves. He doesn't appreciate all this, so he throws himself on the floor, screaming, kicking, and knocking over a vase we held in our own hands all the way across the Atlantic Ocean in a plane from Sevres six years ago.

Suddenly, it's all over, the calm intentions, the promises never to threaten like this, knowing how irresponsible these words are — all shattered like the vase. We shout back, loud and clear, *"Wait 'til your father comes home!"*

That's it. Even when a mother exercises her free will to punish her own child, it must be with *his* authority, carrying out *his* wishes in *his* name.

5

Peer Power

Father and mother stamp their influence very early, and they stamp it hard and deep. But at some stage their authority begins to wane, and a new source of pressure takes over. I call it *Peer Power*.

Parents have been pretty much involved with "What will the neighbors think?" and moved by the well-meaning Emilys of the world who praise our children for being "all boy" and "a little lady." Often, fathers set idealistic goals for their sons and daughters so that a business associate—heaven forbid—will have no reason to doubt junior's masculinity and sister's femaleness. Mothers make sure we keep on our sexist roads. But somewhere, usually starting with the school years, contemporaries gain the edge in influence. By early adolescence, Peer Power is in full force.

In those preteen years, we are usually like columns of jelly, firming but still kind of quivery. We have our directions vaguely set; the goals are in sight. Sometimes we just don't know if we'll ever get there, or even if we want to. Our main goal is to get married and have babies.

My own adolescence was almost a generation ago, but from talking with students today, I am convinced that most girls (though a smaller percentage than in my generation) still feel that some form of marriage is part of their plan. The second aim we have is personal growth in college or career, or both. Girls today are considering blending marriage and a career as part of their total life-style much more than we did. Fifteen years ago, we thought of college and a career in one of two ways—as preparation so we'd have "something to fall back on," or as a way to suitable marriage openings.

I remember, back in the fifties, my freshman high school English teacher, a sensitive and scholarly gentleman, brought me some Barnard College brochures because I had mentioned an interest in someday going there. As I was thanking him, a classmate of mine ambled over.

"What's that you have?" she asked. Then, seeing the title, she grimaced, "Oh, college!"

"You're a bright girl, Pat," Mr. Belvedere told her. "Aren't you thinking about college?"

She answered with the pseudo-confidence of a

nouveau-adolescent echoing her parents, "I'm going to get married anyway. What do I need college for?"

Mr. Belvedere smiled and said, "The better you educate yourself, the more you'll be able to teach your children."

I'm still not sure if Mr. Belvedere was shrewdly trying to convince a bright girl to raise her intellectual standards, or if he really believed that college was useful only in helping her perform as a mother. At any rate, you might have guessed that Pat did not go to college, but found herself a secretarial job shortly after graduating from high school. Within two years, she was progressively "going steady," engaged, and finally blissfully married. Well, married anyway.

Pat's attitude was the culmination of typical parental pressure and Peer Power. Her mother had steered her toward marriage, her father had shown her that men like femininity in a girl. How could advanced education and an aggressive professional career fit into the pattern of ladylike maternal instinct? Peer Power was lending its support with the realization that boys were finally reaching the stage of appreciating girls, and now it was up to the girls to grab themselves one of these guys. And adolescent Peer Power brings on the dawning that it is every girl for herself when it comes to that valuable commodity, a boyfriend.

Although Peer Power eventually crowds out parental influence, it takes a while to really take root. Mother, especially, is still hanging in there, more vocal than ever, as she watches what was not so long ago a dependent toddler now making her way to total womanhood. This is the time when mothers are faced with a conglomeration of contradictory attitudes. On the one hand, they want their daughters to become something special and not fall into that frustrating dependency upon one man. They feel dismay that their bright little girls of sixth grade are becoming lackadaisical in seventh, and by eighth grade, are more content with failing than with succeeding. Suddenly, mother is watching the whole pattern of a young woman suppressing not only her superiority in certain areas but even her equality, and applying a mask of calm adoration just as she applies the mask of makeup she is now allowed to wear.

On the other hand, the mother wants her daughter to be popular, and popularity comes from acting out the traditional female role. It is an emotionally expensive period for both women; mother swings back and forth trying to keep her girl on the track while instinctively wanting to cry out, "Be something more! Don't let yourself fall into this same trap!"

When you were a teenager, you probably heard your own mother complain "You have *got* to get better grades in school." Then she would turn around and gripe "Why are you sitting around with your nose in a book? It's summer; go out and enjoy yourself."

Or, while bestowing one of those motherly lectures about having a boy respect you (of great concern in my teen years), with the next breath, she's urging you to "Put on some lipstick and comb your hair. Look like a girl for a change!"

Father is beginning to waver a bit too. He is watching his dainty daughter subjugating herself to a teenage hero, whom dad feels certain is not worth

her attention. He remembers his own adolescence—
how he was out to make every girl he could get his
hands on, how he practiced looking tough and talking
machismo, and the pride he felt in bringing on the
tears. No, his little girl deserves better than that.

But the pattern has been set, and dad did write
the rules. Daughter is on the warpath for the male
scalp, and it is out of father's hands now. He sold her
an image of dependency, insufficiency, passivity, and
she bought it because nothing else was offered. By the
time they reach high school, girls realize that father
was not the only rule-writer; every man in history has
authored a chapter, and it's best to get on the band-
wagon. It may not be too late for a teenage girl to
change, but for many, there are enough problems
around without tackling this one too.

Slowly and subtly, we begin breaking away from
the preteen gang of girls; we may huddle with one dear
friend for support and understanding, but deep down,
we are all on our own and we know it.

If mother and father are having their second
thoughts about a woman's mythological second nature,
so are daughters. Girls begin categorizing women into
two groups: Mothers, the drag crowd, and Singles, the
fun set.

Our mothers, to us, are totally uninspired and
devoid of glamor, despite the fact that we know this
is where we are headed. Still, for now, husband hunting
is far in the future. We allow ourselves to fantasize
about the gay divorcee, the merry widow, the career
girl—in other words, the Independent. I used to think
of it as the Scarlet O'Hara syndrome.

When I was in high school (you must bear with my reminiscences), my best girl friend and I were told to present a short scene before our drama class. We chose a favorite of all young girls, *Gone With the Wind,* which we were both reading for the third time, once for each time we saw the movie. We decided that one of us would take the part of Scarlet, the other would play Melanie.

Which, of course, brought us to the problem of casting. We both wanted to play Scarlet, as independent a heroine as any girl could hope to find, while Melanie was, in the words of my four-year-old son, "Yuk!"

We argued, we cajoled, we bargained, but neither would back down. Finally, Mickey, in a burst of genius (now that I think of it), put it to me this way: "Let's not do a scene with Melanie. Let's do Scarlet and Prissy coming home to Tara. Prissy has all the good lines; she can roll her eyes and act scared. Scarlet has almost nothing to say."

That did it. Only for the challenge of artistry would I yield the fantasy of Scarlet O'Hara.

Ultimately, however, girls do begin to loosen the cloak of single-woman intrigue. Mother has made the decision that daughter had better settle down to serious husband hunting. Though daughter may say, "I'm not ready to get married yet," her defensiveness runs no deeper than a cape thrown around her shoulders. Once the opportunity for matrimony draws near, she is very quick to fling away that cape and don the shawl of matronhood. After all, it's tiresome to be the outcast in a growing circle of young marrieds.

Peer Power has taken over, for boys as well as girls. Remember the story of *The Graduate?* Poor Benjamin is prodded and coaxed to go into plastics—if not plastics, then anything, as long as it offers a financially secure future. The masculine version of success has nothing to do with marriage. Mother may nag him, "Get yourself a nice wife, son," but she doesn't boast, "My son is married to a bright woman with a good job." Her boasts are more in the vein of "My son, the doctor." Sigh. In fact, she is probably secretly happiest if he's a doctor and not married. But that's another book.

Boys adjust very nicely to girls once they have accepted them, and no wonder. Boys bask in the glory of having some teeny-bopper copy their homework, or ask for help in anything from driving to Dickens. They smile in dazzled amusement as we girls vie among ourselves for their attention. Eventually, the bewilderment turns into acceptance, and finally, girls are taken for granted.

One Saturday afternoon, my neighbor Lois dragged her fifteen-year-old son to the supermarket, where she ran into her daughter's high school teacher. Lois latched on to the teacher with, "What do you think is happening to Fran? Last year she brought home such good grades and now she's barely passing!"

The teacher replied, "Fran's motivation is lost. She's a teenager now, in high school. She sits in class brushing her hair instead of reading her books." But she didn't seem particularly disturbed, concluding, "It's perfectly normal. The girls are more interested in boys now."

Lois' son told me later how he suddenly felt sorry for his sister, because for a brief moment he saw the world from her side, upside down, with girls on the bottom. He envisioned Fran's future as a matrimony-minded file clerk, then housewife, then mother. It made him sad for awhile, because Fran was smarter than he, but then he put it out of his mind, thinking, "That's the way things are. Didn't Mrs. Lewis say that Fran's perfectly normal?"

Fundamentally, this is what inspires Peer Power; as girls are pushed to compete for boys (the boys loving every minute), parents and many teachers beam with approval, and the world cries out, "It's perfectly normal." Except for the girl who just can't get tuned in to boys and only boys; for her, it's disastrous. Peer Power is also boosted by guidance counselors. These people are experts at steering children; they are notorious for telling girls the "best fields" to go into. For example, a girl interested in science is encouraged to forget about chemistry and physics and concentrate on biology, or better yet, nursing. Every girl is advised to take shorthand and typing: "It always comes in handy." And the catch-all for every kind of ability and interest is teaching—art, math, literature, or science—you can *teach* anything.

In my high school, there were three courses of study available to girls. For those aimed at college, there was the academic avenue, where the guidance bees buzzed for nursing, teaching, or even teaching nursing—any combination of these two. For the bright, but no-college-for-me-thanks set, there was straight secretarial.

Finally, for the not-too-bright, not-too-interested group, there was the general course. These girls became literate, but not much more. The guidance counselors wrote them off right away. Their hope was getting husbands to take care of them.

There was no room for humanness or individuality, and things have not changed radically from those years. The basis is the same; even the top high schools are pushing the straight sexist route. If, in a progressive school, a girl is allowed to study mechanical arts, it's so that she can fix the sink when it gets clogged; if a boy takes cooking, it's so he can become a famous chef. In gym, girls are not being taught any athletics other than girls' basketball and volleyball, just as we had fifteen years ago. If she wants more, she's not accepting the feminine role says the guidance counselor.

This separation of male and female athletics begins back in grade school. My own daughter, who happens to be quite agile, came home once with this third grade cheer:

> Boys have the muscles,
> Teachers have the brains,
> And girls have the sexy legs
> To win the games!

Combine this with the lure of cheerleading and batons, and girls quickly learn that their athletic prestige is on the sidelines rather than in the main arena.

Recently, a special committee authorized by the New York State Department of Education studied the results of a program geared towards mixed participation in interschool sports activities. "The program," reported *Medical Tribune,* "turned up no evidence of physical, psychologic, or social harm to either the girl contestants or their male teammates, and no major problems of administrative arrangements or supervision." The athletic teams participated in a variety of sports, including golf, gymnastics, skiing, swimming, cross-country running, and riflery.

We have taken for granted that girls don't want to compete with boys in sports events; that they are happier as cheerleaders or when waving a pom-pom over their heads. Yet, two-thirds of the girls involved in this experiment reported that they wanted the challenge, skill, and competition inherent in a boys' team and obviously missing in a girls' team.

Also missing is recognition of the worth of the girls' athletic teams. Several months ago, a friend's daughter stormed home from school. She was furious, having just attended a special junior high school assembly called to give out sports awards to the most deserving athletes. Male athletes, it turned out.

"But what about *your* basketball team?" my friend asked.

"Do you know what the principal said?" Lucy retorted. "At the end of assembly, after all the guys got their trophies, Mr. Holiday mentioned that if any girls wanted their awards, they could stay after school and meet in Room 103. And when we got there, we didn't receive any trophies, only pieces of paper!"

We are so conditioned to being the second, supportive gender, that we let sex discrimination regulate our lives from birth to death, usually not even questioning the logic of it. I'm sure you've experienced much the same situation as Marie, who told me one November morning how depressed she was about having angered her young fiance's parents the evening before.

"They had this little get-together for Don's father's birthday, and the whole family was there," Marie began. "Naturally, it's expected that the women will say a quick hello and then move into the kitchen. That's how it's always done there. Well, yesterday, I just wasn't in the mood for kitchen gab, but when I started into the living room, Don gave me a little shove toward the kitchen. Then he moved alone into the living room where the other men were talking about last week's election.

"Dammit, that was the moment I first sympathized with Women's Liberation. Here I had been working for one of the presidential candidates all year, throwing myself into his campaign. I had more to offer to that conversation than the rest of those guys put together, but because I'm a woman, politics was not a topic for my brain. Automatically, I'm sent to the kitchen to listen to my future sister-in-law complain about her menstrual cramps.

"Anyway, I hung around but there really wasn't anything for me to do, so I ambled into the living room and inserted myself into their conversation, such as it was. They were such duds, spewing out what Walter Cronkite or the *Daily News* spoon-feeds them at night. They didn't even condescend to talk to little old me. Then, later, I overhead Don's mother whispering to Don that I never help with anything. 'She just wants to sit around with all the men. It's disgusting!' "

"What did Don say?" I asked.

"Nothing at all. But later on he advised me that I should have stayed with the women; it didn't look nice." Marie started to cry. "It didn't seem so important last night, but I couldn't sleep afterwards, and this morning I was just so depressed about my future. I really don't even know if I'm ready to get married anymore, and the wedding is three weeks away."

We have taken our "maternal instinct"—that collection of kitchen and bedroom services—for granted so long that its falsity isn't obvious until some occasion reveals it to us. And then we're lost, constrained by rules we never made and might not even want. We have gone through childhood learning that good girls stay neat, keep quiet, and become little ladies. In adolescence we learn that normal girls automatically know how to fix picnic lunches and cheer for the football team. We are taught that leadership, intellect, or athletic prowess is unfeminine. Somehow, we've grown up finding that our lives are tucked into a chaste white envelope labeled "femininity."

Diana Trilling, in an article for *Saturday Review,* commented, "I myself happen to think, for instance, that although it will indeed be a great day for women when they are appointed to full professorship at our leading universities on the same basis as men, it will be an even greater day for women when right in their own living rooms they are given as much serious attention and credence as men now receive when they pass judgment, especially adverse judgment, on an idea or a person."

Yes, Marie got married as planned, and so do

many of us. With our basic training behind us, we step into that ultimate container called matrimony and it irrevocably strangles us as individuals. The cord is pulled taut and tied, and what results is identity strangulation.

6

Identity
Strangulation

During the periodic ritual of packing and unpacking that my family has undergone during the last ten years, it has become a joke that I first make my mark in any new community as "Jeannine's mother" or "Jason's mom." As soon as the moving van pulls away, my children run outside and scout around for new pals. Later, they point me out to the crowd as their mom— a shadowy curtain-hanger, struggling to balance on some stepladder in the depths of a once-vacant house.

Still later, when my husband's boss is ready to meet the Missus, I abandon my post among the dishes to put in an appearance for approval, and am thereupon promoted (or demoted, depending how you look at it) to "Joe's wife." And it is only after passing through these seemingly unavoidable stages of assimilation that I finally get to be recognized as me, "Elizabeth." It's all good for a joke among the girls, but after the first few rounds we usually replace the belly laugh with a smirk and a shrug, a that's-how-life-is chuckle.

That, my dears, is what I like to call our *Identity Strangulation,* and it all begins with two short words: "I do."

Have you ever noticed those "Most Admired Women" polls and "Best Dressed" lists? Without going into the qualifications of Mamie Eisenhower as the most remarkable woman of the year, Mamie, like Pat Nixon, is simply a reflection of her husband. The "winners" are listed as "Mrs.": Mrs. Dwight D. Eisenhower or Mrs. Richard M. Nixon, rather than Mamie or Pat. They earn the right of recognition without personal achievement. On the "Most Admired Men" lineup, Richard M. Nixon stands alone on his merits; you don't see him noted as "Richard M. Nixon, husband of Pat."

By the same token, women can be damned merely by being the wife of an infamous husband, like Mrs. Lee Harvey Oswald.

This demonstrates one way that marriage causes the strangulation of our identity. It starts with the first chords on the organ as we are escorted down the aisle on daddy's arm. He hands us to Mr. Right, and like property we are moved from one man's jurisdiction to another's. By the time the ceremony is over, we have shed what every person has a right to, one's own name.

Pocahontas ceases being legally known as Pocahontas; she is now Mrs. John Rolfe. In most cases, she is obliged by law to live where John chooses; to have sexual relations with him at his will; and to perform the domestic chores. She belongs to him, not in the romantic way of popular songs but in cold, legalistic terms.

This might be a good place to state that I am not against marriage. At least, not in theory. The commitment of two people to help, support, and love each other could be the straightest road to true liberation there is. It should free us from the burdens of loneliness and frustration so that we might be able to pursue *our* life on *our* terms. But that's the theory. Marriage, as it is structured today, isn't reaching its potential. Somehow, it has become stagnant with outdated expectations and demands, and we waders through life are often strangled by its rigidity. It takes less than $5.00 to get hitched and often more than $1,000 to untie the tangled mess. One out of every three marriages goes kaput. And I'm not even going to try to speculate how many of the remaining two-thirds are satisfactory or relatively happy.

So, the sound of wedding bells fades, the bride's blush pales, the groom's nervousness settles into a little pout, and the marriage is set to begin—life's problems wait to be solved, and the future is ready to be molded.

As far as the groom is concerned, he has gained a dowry dearer than any pot of gold — a combination mistress-housekeeper-social partner-companion and, hopefully, friend. "Friend" is placed last on the list for a good reason; it is the criterion most men would give up first. After all, they can always have a good male friend, someone who shares all those machismo memories, someone who can speak "intelligently" about religion and politics, someone who can be an adequate sportsman or sportswatcher, a pal to play chess or checkers, poker or gin with. A woman is only a woman; a good man is a good friend. So what does a man really want from this brand-new wife? Little enough—simply subjugation.

When a young man marries, he is adding another facet to his life. He becomes a married salesman rather than a single salesman. Yet, he is still Joe Smith, Salesman. His wife has lost something, and has become a part of him, a sort of extra appendage.

Not only does the bride lose her name, but she is encouraged to sacrifice her incentive for self-achievement. If a woman works after marriage, the job is usually a means to some specific purpose—a baby, a house, a trip. In other words, the gravy of life. Gravy is nice, but not necessary, so self-achievement drops one notch. Bread and shelter are the essentials, and it is the husband's job to provide them. Therefore, his achievement is of the utmost importance. You might liken a wife's job to the ones from her teenage days, when she worked summers for extra clothes.

A "Mrs." has no effect on the family status; no matter how fastidious a housekeeper, how successful a teacher, how talented a volunteer leader, society still views you as "Mrs. Joe Smith," the salesman's wife. If your husband is a doctor, your status steps upward; a nightwatchman's Mrs. is lower on the scale. It is with *his* job that your prestige, or lack of it, lies.

In addition, although you watch the TV noon news and read the daily morning papers, if you are a full-time housewife, you probably view the world through your husband's eyes. His relationships and interests in the outside world determine how its activities are interpreted to you. This varies, of course, from family to family, according to education, background, and ability, but across the all-American board, this seems to be how it is.

While marriage adds a new facet to a man's life, for a woman it is a substitution of one life for another—of his life for her's. And her identity sinks deeper and deeper with time. After a stint as "Mrs. Joe Smith," she gives birth to a child and becomes "Jane's mother." Later, she graduates to "Tommy's grandmother."

Many women, admittedly, feel this subjugation is a small matter, being part of what might be called "the marriage contract." After all, hubby's taken on the responsibility of providing for his wife and their family, and that is not a trivial undertaking in today's economy. The least a wife can be expected to contribute is a good home and dedication to the family. Without too much grumbling.

But grumble we do, because somehow our role is not quite adult. The basis of this "contract" (how unromantic can a label be!) is simply finance. In our status/money-oriented society, the emphasis on *materia* has become the zero-in point for so many of our problems — the generation gap, the economy, foreign demands, quests for honesty and idealism, and even the liberation of women. The husband brings home the bacon so he gets the final say.

"My wife's liberated," beams one breadwinner we know. "She's like the entire United States Congress, and all I am is Vice-President. Naturally," he chuckles, "that means in case of a tie, I have the deciding vote."

No matter how egalitarian a couple likes to think themselves—and most couples don't consider themselves fifty-fifty partners at all—there is still a gut feeling that the "deciding vote" belongs to the man because he holds the purse strings. And knowing this, many women dispense very early with even attempting a rational argument and resort to feminine wiles; they reach his heart through whichever route is fastest—sex or stomach. It may work, but it's juvenile and it's degrading.

Of course we rebel. We've always rebelled. We withhold sex. We yell at the children. We have tantrums. We grab the household money and run out on a shopping spree. But before now, you couldn't go to your best friend for sympathy because while she might understand your momentary indiscretion, she would not support you in an all-out revolution. Today, she might; tomorrow, she will.

What we have finally lost is our identity as adults. In return for keeping house and bearing children, we receive financial security, and often that security is doled out to us as an allowance. It is a bit larger, hopefully, than our children's allowance, but it is in the same category—handed over periodically with an admonition to spend wisely.

If we are good and don't squander all our allowance, we are rewarded by being allowed to keep what's left over. But half the fun is taken out of it because we feel guilty about spending the breadwinner's hard-earned bread. We did not earn it. Housework is not on the level of a real job; it is just part of the contract of being mistress-social partner-et cetera. Our allowance is not a fixed salary. It is arbitrary. Therefore, any woman who has been coerced into staying home on today's terms of the marriage contract often feels embarrassed about being "just a housewife." As demanding and important as running a home is, we often feel ashamed of it, so, with an attempt at dignity, we call ourselves "homemakers." As indispensable as this job is, ladies, it's taken for granted by our husbands, by society, and worst of all, by ourselves.

I remember one episode of "I Love Lucy" when Lucy sold her old living room furniture so she could buy a brand-new set. How she maneuvered to keep the news from her husband! When he found out what Lucy had done, raging (but righteous) Ricky punished his wife as he would a child. Her allowance was to be withheld until the furniture was all paid for, and Ricky would keep the new furnishings all locked up until the bill was settled.

Of course, this was a humorous exaggeration, but it would not be funny at all if there were not a generous bit of truth to the plot. Humor springs from truth. In the contract of marriage, we women surrender our identity not only as a separate name and a separate job but as a separate adult as well. And we consider ourselves lucky to do it! Why? Because this is, incredibly, exactly the arrangement every woman is supposed to want. What Women's Liberation believes is that every female should have the option to choose the kind of marriage, if any, which seems best for her as a full person. Who can know, of course, what will eventually turn out to be successful, but if a marriage fails, she will at least have the dignity of knowing she made a rational and free decision as a rational, free adult. And she and her husband can dissolve the marriage with just as much dignity.

For some women, life as a Mrs. is acceptable; for others, a two-career relationship, or no formal marriage at all—or any variation of these options—may be more palatable. As things are now, a woman is considered freaky if she decides not to marry, frigid if she wants no children, and radical if she wants to keep her maiden name.

Why must every bride be pushed into that time-honored routine of housekeeper? Everyone admits it's a never-ending career; while husbands publicly acclaim what a valuable asset a housewife is, I don't know of any who are volunteering for this grand profession. And why should they? A man chooses his job, works his day, and expects a little rest and relaxation at home, with affection and tender loving care when he needs it. The Missus plods on with her job well after the normal eight-hour day for seven days a week, 365 days a year, holidays included.

Webster defines *holiday* as "a day on which one is exempt from one's usual labor." Tell that to a housewife and she'll howl. For her, *holiday* means "immersion in labor." It is a Thanksgiving extravaganza to prepare; Christmas wrappings to clear away before starting on the big feast; New Year's Day to get through like any other—hangover or no; Fourth of

July entertaining; cleaning out the summer cottage; packing for a trip, no matter who's going.

A holiday for the housewife begins weeks before, with pie baking, freezing, inviting, marketing, decorating, explaining once more to the children why all this is going on, and scrubbing the place spotless. It does not slow down for a football game or a parade; it doesn't excuse a career mother (rather, it's her chance to show the world that she's really just as womanly as the full-time housewife); it does not exempt one for fatigue, nor does it distribute its chores. A holiday separates the successful homemaker (she is one who is willing to serve and sacrifice without a whimper) from the failure (the one who wants to celebrate in a restaurant). It gauges feminine usefulness by the perfect turkey. A holiday demands and receives organization, creativity, and stamina.

Of course, we get our thanks. It's always pleasant to receive compliments on a tasty turkey and an imaginative decor. Aren't a few words like "Great meal, honey," followed by a hearty belch, a bargain price for the benefactors to pay? Give the little woman a few pats on the back, some well-chosen gratuities—a bunch of flowers or a box of candy—and that should do it.

This isn't news to most wives. Often when hubby brings you a token surprise, don't you wonder, "What's he up to?" You suspect you're being prepaid or postpaid, for some favor to perform or some mischief already done.

I know what you're going to say. "I don't mind doing things for my family. It's good to be loved."

What you mean is "It's good to be needed."

Of course it is. As long as your total self isn't submerged in another person's needs. There must be enough in it for you so that your life totals up as satisfaction, not servitude. Looking back on a life that was less than personally fulfilling can bring bitterness, especially towards those to whom you were once so dedicated.

Some women argue that there is deep fulfillment in running the perfect home. But is there such a thing as a "perfect home"? And as for the creativity, how long does its gratification last? For the holiday dinner, for instance, you collect exciting recipes, plan a gourmet meal, shop for distinctive ingredients, set the table artistically. At best your husband exclaims over each delectable mouthful, and then it's over. How often have you sighed, "This meal took five hours to prepare and fifteen minutes to eat." Sure, there's creativity in cooking, but it's too ephemeral to dedicate so much energy to, year after year, largely for the glory of tradition.

It's similar with decorating your home. Once the furniture is placed and the draperies hung, there's only the upkeep to be bothered with. *Only* the upkeep, did I say? We must admit that the "creativity" involved in waxing the wood, changing the slipcovers, shampooing the rug, and hanging the Indian corn is important for only the few moments it takes one to admire the glowing splendor.

For more and more women, this form of occupational therapy is just not enough. They have found that housekeeping is a functional necessity with its own value, but it must be made part of a meaningful life by combining it with other activities. Outside work may be the answer for some—volunteer, part-time, or full-time. And for the others who still choose the home, well, it should be their choice, made without accompanying feelings of guilt and inferiority. That's what Women's Liberation is about.

Critics say we have a free choice, but we have seen how growing up, in itself, has muddled us, and how society and family influence us. For example, suppose you are a housewife and you want to go out to work; however, your children are still preschoolers. You love those children, you enjoy them, but in regulated doses. You find that toward four in the afternoon, you are snapping at them unfairly. When your husband turns the doorknob at five, you and the kids leap on him, competing for his attention. You, an adult, want to relate all that trivia left over from the day which the children can't appreciate, like the dishwasher making a funny noise and the front door creaking. Sometimes, you optimistically try to discuss what you heard in snatches on the noon news.

"Did the Mideast flare up again? I was in the kitchen fixing lunch so I didn't catch too much. What happened?"

Abby found herself in this situation, pathetically pining for adult conversation. Her husband's attention was divided into many pieces every night: one was grabbed by the older children's first grade and kindergarten adventures; another piece turned toward the baby's yelp; still, a third to the dog's wiggling welcome; and only a slice was left for Abby's news about the neighborhood. Will wondered if this peaceful-home-and-hearth business was all it was cracked up to be. And it was he, in fact, who finally approached Abby about getting herself a job.

"Do you mean it?" Abby cried. Then, fervently, she added, "But the children . . . Danny's only fifteen months old, and Jackie just started kindergarten. Who can I get to baby-sit?"

That, of course, took applied searching, but a sitter was found, paid handsomely, and the children went on with their adventures and yelps. Abby now gets home from work just after her older child gets home from school. She spends the late afternoon talking with the children and fixing supper, and later, she dines alone with her husband. For now they have things to talk about.

Abby's husband is atypically understanding. He did, after all, have to take on some share of the household chores. Abby's wages did not add to the income after child-care, working wardrobe, and commuting expenses were deducted. Yet, he obviously thinks of his wife as an equal rather than as a junior partner, and is willing to give up some of those cherished male prerogatives for her.

(Quite a different attitude has David Susskind, pundit-in-residence of televisionland. Speaking of his wife to Diana Lurie of *New York Magazine* in 1970: "She's my most treasured possession. I possess her. I have her. Nobody else has her. No other male." Poor scared Susskind.)

Where is it written that a good marriage hinges on the wife making the family happy and the husband making the bank happy? This is not to say that some marriages don't work well this way; but it is obvious that there's a need to slice through many generalities, especially those which pin women down in a rut they may not want to be stuck in.

In most families, housework is still the feminine domain. If you and your husband both work, it is probably your job to run from office to kitchen while your husband veers for the martini pitcher. He may help out with a little piano moving, but it is your responsibility to have the house spotless, the children well-adjusted, and everyone fed. Naturally, if it gets to be too much, you know what goes first, and if you don't agree to quit the job, concerned voices chime in from all corners to make sure the point is driven home.

"We don't need your salary," your husband will announce. Can you blame him? It's probably easier for him to give up the extra money than to submerge himself in the drudgery of dishes every night and other chores after the kids go to bed.

"A woman's place is in the home," reiterates your mother, meaning that you are not an individual, but merely part of that large paperdoll category called Womanhood. *A* woman, in other words, rather than *one* woman.

What if you feel *your* place could be at that stimulating job you've been offered? Or what if you don't want to give up those extra dollars each week? What do you do? Two to one, you grit your teeth and mutter to your would-be employer, "Thanks, but no thanks. My family comes first."

And society smiles on you. This is, surprisingly

enough, almost a totally American viewpoint. People in other developed countries routinely employ day-care centers or family members to care for the children. In Italy, where I lived for several years, day-care centers —city run, private, or company sponsored—were commonplace for the youngest children.

Many homes included *nonna,* a grandmother, who lived with her middle-class children, watching the grandchildren while daughter-in-law went off to work. And Italy has not been known, historically, for sex-equality. (However, recently, a series of family laws were passed reforming the archaic customs of child marriages, dowries, and the yielding of a woman's name after marriage. As one legislator put it, "human and social principles" have taken over.)

In Abby's case, she naturally feels the physical strain of two responsibilities. Even gravy isn't all cream and spices. After all, she has part of the housework to keep her from relaxing at night, and she retains her hang-ups about the children being with a sitter all day. This baby-sitter is a woman who has proven herself very capable, but even so, Abby insists, because of her built-in feminine insecurity, a baby-sitter cannot possibly give the children the love that their mother can.

By admitting that a baby-sitter might actually take better care of our children than we could, we are giving up that I-must-be-needed complex. Yet, in many cases, a baby-sitter might do a better job. There is really nothing more we can accomplish for our son's sniffles than the baby-sitter can. And there are even instances where a hired person (how unmaternal that reads) might do a better job than the natural mother; she might be a lot more patient coloring with the bed-ridden child, watching cartoons, and squeezing lots of fresh juices. The mother may have her mind on that office desk that needs clearing off, or on her other children, or she may just be "pooped."

Incidentally, is there any reason why father can't stay home from work occasionally? There are certain days when men are not particularly busy at work. If this is editor-mother's day to get out that magazine, and father can rearrange his business appointments, why can't he stay home with his sick child?

This sort of thinking, of course, requires a complete turn about of attitudes. To be liberated, gals, you are going to have to become openly selfish. When you think about *you,* honestly and candidly, you will begin liberating yourself, and as a result, you will begin liberating your family.

Of course, there are always roadblocks. When your husband occasionally pitches in with the children, everyone heaps the accolades upon him. "That Joe Smith is a great father. He always takes his kids out on weekends, to the zoo, the museums, the movies." However, let Joe beome an actual housework-partner, and the accolades turn to acrimony. He begins to hear things like "Who wears the pants in your family?" It takes a strong ego to deal with that.

Not every woman is naturally maternal, just as every man is not a Hugh Hefner (thank God!). Many husbands enjoy spending lots of time with their children, yet the pressures of modern society keep them away three-quarters of the day. Children could benefit immensely from real attention from daddy. My husband, for example, has infinitely more patience than I when it comes to working with our children. He taught them to read and write before they entered school. He reads them stories and acts out Shakespearean plays for them. While I work at my desk, he takes them out for snowman construction. At times, he prepares dinner when he'd rather be reading the newspaper, just as I often cook when I've got a yen for gardening. We have the special closeness that comes from doing things for each other, not because society says I must cook and he must fix the plumbing, but because we respect each other as whole and variable individuals. But, this turnabout did not come automatically; we talked and we argued. We labored through the entire "You think *you* have it tough! Let me tell you what *I've* been doing all day" routine! (We still resort to that, but not so often anymore.)

Each member of a marriage gets into a rut at times, and each needs a break from it. If husbands and wives could recognize the drudgery each is involved in so much of the day, purely for traditionally sexist reasons, they might provide these breaks for each other. But society tells us that a man who does feminine work is emasculated. (My husband thinks housework is boring, and thus, out of compassion, gives me a hand when necessary—not in the form of a favor, but as a function of our commitment to each other.)

A full-time job is not the answer for every woman. If her husband will not accept part of her home burden, or if she cannot afford household help, she has just added more work to an already over-full day. But even if a woman is the most dedicated home-and-hearther, she'll admit that happiness is often just a free day of shopping, unfettered by fists clinging to her skirt and a cluttered stroller that keeps her out of most crowded places.

A woman's life-style in today's world is inconsistent with the world's demands. Compare the female's life with a male's: His life is a steady progression from childhood to manhood to old age, gaining momentum and importance with each step. It is a logical mounting to whatever height he wants and can achieve.

We women live in stages, each distinct and each separated from the other with a pause: Childhood, adolescence, college or career — stop — marriage, pregnancy, child-rearing, menopause—stop. Life for a woman is a road full of obstacles and detours.

Unfortunately, women are educated in a contradictory way, urged to study higher mathematics and literature, and then told to dump the whole thing for twenty years for marriage and children. Next comes the emptying of the nest. Today, if the older woman wants to get out and continue her life, she is forced to turn around and grope backwards some twenty years to pick up what pieces were left back there, somehow mold them together, and make a new life at forty-five or fifty.

Psychiatrist Bruno Bettelheim claims that many mothers-in-law spoil their grandchildren excessively in their need to recapture their own young motherhood. Often granny feels that her grown children owe her their lives; this is because she gave up her personal aims for her children rather than incorporating her children into the totality of her goals. If a woman had the alternatives a man has when making a choice early in life, she could determine what road she wants to take and what place marriage and children will have along this road. Then later, perhaps, she will not be filled with resentments and yearnings to go back. For we never can go back.

Our children are not responsible for us. If we demand that they be, we become burdens. Life is too short, and old age too long, for us to be millstones. Let's liberate our children by liberating ourselves.

W. B. Yeats wrote:

> Things fall apart, the centre cannot hold;
> Mere anarchy is loosed upon the world, . . .

If we apply the images and ideas in these lines to the family, with the mother the "centre," then the power and responsibility we have is indeed heady. This is the way many of us view ourselves. But, in reality, we are not all that powerful or important—our families will not "fall apart" without us (although they may rattle a bit). The best thing we can do for our families is to provide a firm base, which we can do most effectively when we stand strong, with our own potential met.

If you have your own identity, your own life, you will not have to become a "Tommy's grandmother," a nagging mother-in-law, or a free, ever-available baby-sitter. Wouldn't it be pleasant to slip into the role of grandparent simply and naturally? To help your daughter-in-law with her first dinner party and never mention later how "without me your party would have flopped"? To fly to Connecticut to stay with the kiddies while parents fly off to a business-vacation in Paris? Wouldn't it be admirable to donate your experience without a behind-the-scenes IOU to be "collected" later? If you can keep your own identity through life, if you have your own goals and ambitions and incorporate your family into them, in later years you will not flit aimlessly from hairdresser to gynecologist, a burden to your still active husband, with no real purpose except killing time. Then later, if your husband should die, you will not need to transfer the load of *you* to your children.

Let's be honest: Women's Liberation is grinding out a better life for future wives and mothers within a whole new framework of marriage. We see it with the young women today.

Almost twenty years ago, college alumnae who were asked to choose a pattern of life replied en masse, "Home, with some outside interests." Ten years later, this was changed to "I want to have a career with just a little time out for family." Today, rather than a generation gap, we seem to have a sibling gap on our hands. Sisters of the sixties are just not thinking like their older sisters of the fifties, nor like those of the seventies either. As was pointed out back in 1966, graduating women were opting for work. "The career drive exceeds the mating drive." And as more and more women strive for knowledge, more and more are dissatisfied with the traditional look for today's marriage scene. Your daughter may be among them: She knows that what makes her a woman is not her man.

7

I Am a Woman

Sounds simple, doesn't it? What are you if not a woman? But with all this women-don't-do-that-sort-of-thing and it-isn't-feminine mythology, maybe it's time we pause in our strike for status and glance back at the basics. What, exactly, is femininity? What does being a woman really mean? And how does "femininity" keep us from achieving?

Corporate medical advisor of International Paper Company, Dr. Mildred E. Ward, posed the same question when she remarked in *Medical World News:* "A few years back, I was severely criticized by a surgeon who did not know me and did not know whether I was a good or bad surgeon. He stated flatly that a woman is not capable of doing surgery. So I went and found him, and I said, 'Doctor, I want to watch you operate. I want to see what part of your anatomy you use in performing surgery that I as a woman am not equipped with.' "

Besides the obvious primary and secondary sex characteristics (as the high school biology textbooks put it), what is it that *they* have and *we* don't—and vice versa—that guarantees this primary position they hold. Women have been considered the "second sex" throughout history on two fundamental counts, physical and intellectual. The female body has been poised on a towering pedestal for centuries, and is still there despite the recent leaning toward erotica.

The female body has been worshipped, deified, scandalized, and debased. Women themselves have experimented with its health by swallowing unproven birth control pills, and have changed its contours with nips, tucks, and silicone. No one has yet given a sound scientific reason for relegating woman's body to second place, behind the "superior" male. No one can simply because there *is* no reason, only myths, and, as we said before, decay is setting in on them.

Female, then, is most succinctly defined as the sex having the potential for menstruation, pregnancy, parturition, and lactation. And that, ladies, is it.

These four processes are the result of a collection of tissues, internal and external, called the Reproductive System, which is basically what separates the boys from the girls. The potentiality of menstruation, et al., is what constitutes the quality of our "femininity," but this potential should not be expanded to become our total humanness.

Internally, the reproductive organs are situated within the pelvis, a bony basin-like structure. Of course, both sexes have pelves, but yours is shallower and more delicate than your husband's, and the "basin" itself is wider (all the better to hold a growing fetus). It's a supremely strong structure, harder than the skull or the chest. The four bones that form it are the hipbones on both sides and in front, and the sacrum and coccyx in back.

Even among women, pelves differ. In fact, short women usually have broad pelves, which might surprise those people who always fret for the tiny girl who finds she is pregnant.

"Where will she put that baby?" they wonder.

Well, there's room.

The basin shape of the pelvis is very practical because it holds the internal female organs—ovaries, uterine (or Fallopian) tubes, uterus, and vagina. These are necessary to carry out our part in reproduction, and three-quarters of our four-point definition of female is centered right here. And like a machine, the feminine foursome is geared to begin action at a certain time—which we call puberty. Menstruation signals the start of adult womanhood.

From prenatal days, girls surge ahead of boys. We live longer both in and out of the womb; in fact, within every age group, more males die than females. Child psychiatrists agree that little girls talk sooner, toilet train faster, adjust to school more quickly, and are often larger than their male playmates.

As we approach puberty, our growth quickens; we shoot up, fill out, and eat up a storm. Then we have our first period, and everything slows down. By then, we pretty much have our adult height and shape, although the whole process varies a great deal from girl to girl. From then on, we get sick more often than men, but we also recover much faster, and as far as succumbing to illness, we surpass men only in fatal reproductive ailments. Men are "weaker" as regards withstanding illness in every other area, including hereditary ailments, ulcers, and gout.

Whether this is by nature or not is still speculative, although some experts feel it might go back to our chromosomes. At any rate, there is nothing about our feminine processes which indicates inferiority of any degree.

The female pelvis holds two pinkish-gray ovaries, each of which lies in a little niche in the pelvis. These ovaries produce eggs. In childhood, ovaries are smooth, but with menstruation they become progressively more convoluted, until by menopause they are puckered, shrunken, and nonfunctioning.

Inside each ovary are many round transparent follicles, some of which contain the developing eggs. In a newborn baby girl, there are about half-a-million follicles present in the two ovaries. During the child-bearing years, about 385 of these follicles grow and expel their eggs. Many eggs never mature (lucky for us; at that rate, the population would have exploded many times over). In fact, only one egg matures during each menstrual cycle. Out of these only a few are ever fertilized.

Menstruation is a part of a cycle which repeats itself over and over until a point in one's life—during middle age—when the cycle ceases. This is called menopause. At a certain time in the cycle, one of the ovarian follicles moves up to the surface of the ovary and bursts, sending its liberated egg into the Fallopian tube and down to the uterus. Once this is done, the follicle folds up into the space once taken by the egg; this filling is called the *corpus luteum.* Hormones are secreted which inhibit the release of any more eggs, as well as stimulate the growth of the mammary glands and the implantation of the fertilized egg in the uterine wall to grow. These two action hormones are estrogen and progesterone. Without them female reproductive organs would not develop and function normally.

Once the egg is released from the ovary, it moves into the thin, muscular duct leading to the uterus; this is the Fallopian tube. Within this tube is the liaison spot for sperm and egg. The result of this meeting is usually fertilization. If a newly fertilized egg does not move on into the uterus, a tubal pregnancy occurs which must be terminated, since the five-inch-long tube cannot hold a growing embryo for very long.

The uterus is a hollow, muscular, pear-shaped organ lying between the bladder and the rectum (not a very romantic spot for the growing offspring!). If the egg has been fertilized, it attaches to the wall of the uterus. Immediately this organ begins to change so that it can care for the new embryo. The uterus feeds and protects this growing embryo for nine months, enlarging itself thirty times, until the baby is expulsed. Then the uterus shrinks to about twice its prepregnancy size. After menopause, the uterus begins to shrivel, and by old age, it may be the size of a thumb.

If the egg is not fertilized, the entire preparation for the egg is undone, and this is menstruation. The progesterone supply is cut off. The inner lining of the uterus begins to shed in patches, for it is no longer needed. (Many medical men, and millions of women, are now recognizing the problem of this continual building up and tearing down, along with the premenstrual headaches, irritability, nausea, and fatigue that often accompany menstruation.)

At the bottom of the uterus is a constricted opening called the cervix which leads to the vagina, a four-inch-long corridor leading from the uterus to the exterior of the body. At the door of the vagina is a thin, circular fold of mucous membrane called the hymen, the so-called proof of virginity. This is the "skin" which many teenagers used to be afraid of rupturing by horseback riding or motorcycling. Another myth, for many times it is so flexible as to remain intact even after intercourse. (Some "virgin births" were debunked when they were found to be based on the hymen being still intact.)

The vagina acts as a receptacle for the penis and the ejaculate. From here, the sperm moves toward the Fallopian tubes where fertilization takes place. At childbirth, the vagina serves as a birth canal for the emerging fetus. Childbirth demands a great deal of give in the vaginal wall; the muscles dilate in order to accommodate the fetus. But after birth, even if things are never quite the same with those walls, the vagina does contract again to almost its prenatal state.

The external parts of the reproductive system can be included under one umbrella name, the *vulva*. This is a rather involved area which includes first of all the labia majora, two elongated folds which surround a cleft. It is into this cleft that the urethra and the vagina open. This area is abundant with glands, many of which secrete lubricants to facilitate intercourse.

Two smaller folds are found inside the labia majora; these are called, sensibly enough, labia minora. Near the front of these folds is found the clitoris, the vital sensuous zone of a woman's body.

Many woman feel that the vagina is the female counterpart of the male penis. Not so; the clitoris is the most sensitive of a woman's sexual regions—the part that, when stimulated, brings the most sexual satisfaction to a woman. The clitoris is formed somewhat like a very small (women experts might say "refined") penis, and capped by the tiny, highly responsive *glans*. But unlike the penis, the clitoris is anchored and comparatively immobile.

While three-quarters of our feminine foursome are found in the pelvic region, the fourth, lactation, involves the mammary glands in the breasts. Although the main function of the mammary glands is to nourish the young, history has placed the satisfaction of food appetite second to the satisfaction of sexual appetite, as far as a woman's breasts are concerned. Breasts today are a tremendously profitable part of our culture, influencing entertainment, fashion, and advertising.

But back to nourishment: During pregnancy, the area around the nipples darkens, the breasts swell, and the milk ducts enlarge so they can provide the new baby with all the food it demands. After the baby is weaned, the mammary glands get smaller, the milk ducts return to their former size, and the space they once took up is filled with fat tissue. If you've always believed that a mother's breasts are smaller and flabbier than those of a woman who has never given birth, you are right. In addition, the pigmentation acquired in pregnancy never fades completely.

So there lies femininity. The body of a woman is constructed, physically and hormonally, to protect and nurture this new human individual, that's true. But it's also true that we are constructed for many other purposes as well, since we bear only limited numbers of children during our lifetime (and our zero-population-minded daughters will bear even fewer). Therefore, giving birth and nursing is only a segment of our lives, so our value as people should not be limited by the boundaries of the reproductive organs.

We must agree that men have larger bones and muscles, but women are far from being the weaker sex. Men, unfortunately, have used their larger muscles to place us in a weaker position. In *The Natural Superiority of Women,* Ashley Montagu states: "Because, by virtue of his greater physical power, man has been able to determine the fate and development of woman, men and women have come to assume that it was natural for men to do so, and both have come to mistake their prejudices for the laws of nature. . . . Female subservience is a culturally, not a biologically, produced condition. It is one of the consequences of the misuse of masculine power."

Men generally are larger, have a higher metabolism rate, and eat more than women. Do these biological differences mean that they also, by nature, have more drive and ambition, and enjoy greater sexual drive? Does it follow that the husband must earn the bread if he has larger biceps? Or that he cannot feel secure and let his wife work if she is the more aggressive partner? Destroying stereotypes can only benefit wives and husbands; it can only free both sexes to enjoy their individual capabilities.

There is little need for heavy musculature in today's automated world. Simone de Beauvoir put it quite succinctly in *The Second Sex*: "Abundance [of musculature] makes for superiority only in the perspective of a need, and to have too much is no better than to have enough. Thus the control of many modern machines requires only a part of the masculine resources, and if the minimum demanded is not above the female's capacity, she becomes, as far as the work is concerned, man's equal."

During the Civil War and World War I, women were called out of their Victorian restraint to join the workforce, replacing the fighting men. And replace them they did, from farm to factory, labor pool to executive desk. If, at the beginning, women's competency was viewed by men with hesitation, women must have done something right, for, in the next great war, back again they were called. This time with no hesitation at all.

Yet, once the crisis was passed, and men marched back to their jobs, back went the temporarily liberated women to the washline with songs of joy about returning to the wonderful life of the "everyday house-wife."

You may wonder why a woman should want to do heavy physical labor, even if she is capable of doing it. One answer is money. A strapping young gal can make a much larger salary handling a cement mixer than she can pounding a typewriter.

How about those hormones? you ask. Don't they keep us weaker, especially during menstruation? Menstruation may be a "pain" in certain areas, but usually it is not an incapacitating physical pain. It's not the "curse" we have been taught to regard it as. Most of us accept the onset of menstruation with a mixture of pride and apprehension, but not with the fear our grandmothers felt. It is only after years of reading, talking, and learning that we begin to despise it and having to put up with it. Menstruation, however, usually has no detrimental effect on our productivity. Most of us, if we are busy, are usually surprised that it is "that time of the month" again. In today's tampon world, menstruation as a "curse" is just another fable.

As for hormones, many medical experts believe that they may actually shield us from heart disease. We all know that men are more susceptible than women to heart ailments, either because of male hormones or a more hectic, competitive life, or both. Women, how-ever, become just as susceptible after menopause, or after the ovaries are removed in surgery, which means that the workings of her sex hormones have ceased.

Is pregnancy a deterrent to work? We all probably know of women who have chosen to work almost up to their delivery date; and we've heard about the women who must labor in rice paddies until the first pangs of labor. After all, if we take our vitamins, get a sensible amount of sleep, and eat nutritious food, we can do no more for the embryo within us. We can't regard being pregnant as a creative activity, anymore than we can say becoming pregnant is solely a feminine accomplishment. Nursing the baby does belong only to the mother, but even with the most "natural" of mamas, lactation lasts only a few months.

Finally, parturition demands some rest, at least in our society. But any mother having her second or third child knows that when she gets home from the hospital, chances are she's back to busy-ness. Even with live-in help, she will have plenty of tasks to tackle, be it cleaning, cooking, washing, shopping, caring for older children, caring for the newborn; well, you get the picture. Is going back to housework so much easier than going back to office work? For some women, yes. For others, no. To each her own, right?

Perhaps the whole proof of this particular pudding can be found in the space flights, symbol of the seventies.

Why are there no space women? is the question.

Why indeed? In simulated space flights, women showed better orientation and handling of controls, and NASA has cited that they would probably endure the psychological hazards of space flight better than men. But our society isn't ready for that. Russia takes advantage of her woman-power, but we don't. It's hard to believe that there are absolutely no women in America who might *like* a crack at an astronaut's career. Don't women, if capable, deserve the chance to participate in the most challenging work of our times?

We have been kept in second place intellectually, as well as physically. How is it that our daughters who have such a head start at birth become "illogical" and "unreasoning" at adolescence? Could it be that we tell them they'd better stay dumb if they want to get a man? So they let the guys surge ahead, help build their egos, and root from the sidelines as they take the lead in running things for their generation.

Psychologists agree that there is no conclusive evidence that men have innate intelligence for problem-solving, while women are "intuitive." Why is it that women are "biologically predestined" to prepare food in the home while the great chef positions are held by men? Why do women sew and mend for their families while the crème of the famous couturiers are usually men? How come women are naturally "romantic" but the great Romantic poets were, you guessed it, male? And why is it that women are "born with a love for curls and frills," but the most elegant period of history was the English Restoration, when men in ruffles abounded.

This is not to say that we should each go our separate way, wipe the slate clean of sexual differences, and embrace a world of unisex. We are necessary to each other. After all, that egg, if not united with a male sperm, will just be washed away in menstruation. We could not grow a fetus within us or deliver an infant or nourish a baby at our breast if there were no man to help start it all. Part of femininity might never flourish without its masculine counterpart.

Then again, this might not matter to many women. Just as there are many men who never father children, yet are fulfilled and considered masculine, there are many women who never give birth and yet feel perfectly fulfilled as human beings and completely feminine. Parenthood is *part* of living, not the *raison d' etre*. And when society accepts this for women as well as for men, the quality of life will be improved for everyone—most of all, perhaps, for children.

We have seen how the terms *masculinity* and *femininity* have encompassed a cobweb of meanings. Their original biological basis has been obscured, and replaced by fables such as masculine aggressiveness, creativeness, productiveness, and action versus feminine gentility, stability, and passivity. In the twentieth century, we can easily switch these sexual descriptions, and give to those women who are capable the virtue of aggressiveness, and to those men who deserve it the label of gentility. Often the two mix happily.

But to do it, we have to shake up society a bit. Just as the most deeply-Southern of Dixie's gentlemen are beginning to acknowledge the humanness of blacks, so will the most extreme male chauvinist learn to accept the humanness of women. The next generation will open their minds a little wider, but we must never forget that the prejudiced (against women as against blacks, Puerto Ricans, or the next minority in line) do not accept the object of their prejudice voluntarily. They need the prodding of the unified strength of organizations. They react to the threats of extremists. And they bow finally to the stipulations of law. Why? Because reason will eventually decree that discrimination is wrong, impractical, and useless. There is no pragmatic reason why women should hang on to the myth of a three-steps-behind, clinging-vine brand of femininity.

As our environment throughout the ages has determined the roles we have played, so it must continue to determine our roles today—individually, woman by woman. What was needed in the hunt-and-fight pioneer days is not necessary in today's push-button, laminated, formica-top world. It's time we accepted that.

Femininity is an anatomical and physiological quality; it is not an emotional nor intellectual state. Therefore, it cannot be "lost" (except, perhaps, through surgery that changes one's gender). Yet, we are indoctrinated into believing we can "lose" our femininity by sitting at the executive's desk, manipulating at a political caucus, or even playing on a football field. Impossible.

It is just as impossible to "lose" our femininity in the bedroom by veering from accepted roles. American society today is tackling its sex hangups. Isn't it time the real American woman (the one who doesn't live on the TV or movie screen, in best-seller novels, or in the slick pages of *Cosmopolitan* magazine) starts tackling hers?

8

Sex and the
Liberated Housewife

Once upon a time there was something called the "double standard." This meant that a man was supposed to want, need, and deserve sex, and it was up to the woman to provide it. However, an interest in sex was believed to go against a woman's innately higher moral character; the woman who liked and wanted sex was a bad apple in the saintly barrel of womanhood.

The peak of this line of thought was reached less than a hundred years ago, when Victorian Age men were convinced that when they felt the need for a certain sort of satisfaction, they were to go out and sow their oats. Women, on the other hand, were correct to remain chaste, not only until marriage but after. Sex was for procreation, not pleasure. If a damsel resorted to flirtation and levity to catch her gent, she was to cool off and stand respectable once he was caught. So the nineteenth century gentleman placed his stone bride on a pedestal, showered her with sentimental valentines, and took his passion elsewhere.

In those pre-Portnoy days, propriety went so far as to suggest that men and women visit museums separately for fear the classical nudes might prove embarrassing in mixed company. That was the era for sewing little trousers for one's piano legs (oops, *limbs*). Huckleberry Finn was a dirty young man in the 1880s, and the waltz threatened ruination to the few young ladies daring enough to try it.

It took World War I to start society hacking at this marble pedestal, and fifty years later, it finally collapsed in a thunderous, frightening crash. In "How You Gonna Keep 'Em Down on the Farm," *'em* referred not only to the returning doughboys but to their American lasses waiting on the dock. Contraceptives were cheap and plentiful (if on the primitive side by today's pop-the-pill standards). The automobile offered privacy and the movies showed that even the Celluloid beauties were doing it.

Yet, this cropping of hair, lifting of skirts, smoking, drinking, and shimmying was all in fun, in the spirit of kids who are turned loose in a toy store. It lasted until the Depression, which was followed by World War II, and then almost immediately by another war in Korea, by bombs, affluence, the pitiable grasping for security led by Senator Joseph McCarthy and for prosperity with General Eisenhower. Finally, we were hit by the explosion of pollution, assassinations, riots, destruction, and incredibly, still another war in the 1960s—and what started out to be gentle chipping away at unnatural restrictions on a natural feeling turned into frantic, quixotic desperation. What amused Scott Fitzgerald yesterday is horrifying Norman Mailer today. What was innocent revelry for the Flappers is perversion in the Synthetic Seventies. Today's women have not only leaped off that uncomfortable pedestal but have been handed sex, brazen and candid, on a satin pillow. And what was once merely an offer of some of the sensual fun has become a desperate demand for the omnipotent, benevolent orgasm.

And where has it left women? Has this long-term sexual revolution freed them? In a way, not at all. Even that ultimate of liberations, the easy-to-take birth control tablet, has lifted the last shreds of responsibility from the shoulders of men—it has made more women more available. In addition, this revolution has divided women into groups. There are many women who still believe that sex belongs where it always was, within the bounds of matrimony. Our primary role, they say, aside from conception, is pleasing our mates.

However, there are growing numbers of women who have grabbed that satin pillow bestowing sexual satisfaction and won't do with less than the best. It has all led to a lot of frustration for a lot of females. Suddenly we are being told to demand varied, experimental sex to please us as well as men. We can be aggressive in bed and still remain feminine. Now, we not only are allowed to abandon our passivity but are informed that we are backward dolts if we don't. All of a sudden, after eons of gentility, we hear, "You've come a long way, baby. Let loose and enjoy it."

Easier said than done.

Psychiatrists have noted three distinct phases in this revolution, characterized by the sexual difficulties described by patients. The first phase was marked by wives who came in to moan about their husbands' excessive sexual demands. Next in time came the husbands, wondering what was wrong with their wives, who were not reaching the orgasms they should. And today, wives are back again, griping that something is wrong with the way their husbands go about love making; we, the wives, just aren't reaching the orgasms we're entitled to!

In a recent nationwide survey, 2,338 women responded as follows to the question, "What do you like least about the sexual aspect of marriage?" Only ten percent mentioned no complaints at all. Thirty-three percent answered that there were too many foreplay or oral-anal demands from their husbands. (Interestingly, this was the most common complaint among the under thirty-five age group.) Seventeen percent responded that they disliked the "messiness" most (very common among the over-fifty crowd). Sixteen percent of the women reported "no orgasm"; and twelve percent complained that their sex life was "routine and unimaginative." The remaining twelve percent gave a variety of answers.

What this survey seems to point out is that women are becoming more verbal about pinpointing specific short-comings in their husbands with regard to sex.

Gone is the feeling that husbands are asserting some inbred right against the will of their submissive wives. In fact, the "men have a stronger sex drive than women" myth is pretty well buried by today's females.

In the next few years, one can predict more break-ups in marriages because of sexual incompatibility. This can mean failure of the woman to reach orgasm every time, or an inability of the man to maintain an erection. Our demands for absolute climactic satisfaction keep mounting, and we seem to have forgotten the concept of giving and receiving love and tenderness, which is essential for both sexes. There is no sex "role" in bed, after all, only two distinct human beings with individual needs, desires, and love feelings.

Many sociologists and psychiatrists explain this trend by remarking that the housewife role society has pressured women into offers so little other excitement that we embrace every lure to sexual romance offered. We send away for Hollywood nighties, bust hormone creams, how-to and what-not-to-do manuals. If nothing else, it is all supposed to help us keep what husbands we have. Harsh as these words sound, they may well spell out one reason for female insatiability for the romantic sex in books, movies, and magazines.

Though they are the prime market for romantic adventure stories, women until very recently eschewed hard-core sex tales. Jacqueline Susann and Harold Robbins wrote for the housewife, but Terry Southern (*Candy*) did not. However, with the success of the all-you-want-to-know-about-sex and the how-to-be-a-sensu-ous-woman interpretations of love making, more and more women are becoming less interested in adventure with sexual highlights, and more amenable to pornography. Always tuned in to women's buying trends, films have been moving in, turning their leading ladies' desires from love to sex, steering hard-sex past the censors, the prudes, the religious leaders, and "nice" middle-Americans.

This movement could be sensed in the film *Lovers and Other Strangers,* where the wife claims that her tired husband owes her three orgasms already and he'd better start paying up. This is making love? Contemporary film heroes suggest mechanized computers, programmed for body science. They encourage their audience to develop the syndrome of orgasm worship.

Orgasm worship has ordered the conversion of a bedroom into an orgasm workshop, stocked with technique manuals, tools, and know-how. Husbands have their very definite part to play, unlike the good old days when all a man needed was an erection and if there was any inadequacy in the conjugal bed, it was feminine in form. Just as sex has divided womankind, it has done the same for men, as proven by a Masters and Johnson report that correlated a man's educational level with his concerns about satisfying his wife's sexual needs:

"High-school dropouts rarely complain about premature ejaculation although their wives may. . . . Men whose educational level is higher, and whose sophistication is greater, are more likely to feel that their masculinity is threatened by failure to satisfy their wives."

In addition, no two people, no matter how closely entwined are their educational, religious, and moral levels, and no matter how content they are with each other, can have identical sexual patterns and peaks. So how can each partner expect maximum satisfaction every time? Yet, we are being told to demand just this, and keep at it until we are technically proficient, to abandon ourselves totally, and dedicate ourselves to that desperate quest for what may well be an impossible dream.

So, here we are. Where once truly feminine women were supposed to be above having an interest in sex, today they are expected to be possessed by it. Those men most threatened by Women's Liberation will yell out as a final retort, "All you need is a good screw!" and believe our "little rebellion" will be squelched. The myth has been turned topsy-turvy, and somehow women again come out the losers. Whether repressed or possessed, we are neurotic and we need help.

What we do *not* need, surely, is more technical lessons from male "experts." Today's sex manuals give us such detailed instructions on what to do and how to do it that many women find themselves concentrating on techniques rather than on expressing desire and love. A vicious circle is generated when we try to control our love-making by manipulating it. We have difficulty reaching a point of abandonment, that stage which is essential to reaching the climax. We aim for simultaneous, multiple, and prolonged orgasms and feel cheated, embarrassed, and inadequate if we don't achieve them.

Yet, the orgasm for women is complex and very much more than a series of physical vaginal sneezes. It is based largely on psychological factors. You may have experienced the feeling of being close to that point of no return when something happened—the phone rang, or the cat ran across the bed, or the heat valve shut off with a slam—and the mood was lost.

Even for today's modern adult, orgasm is not predictable. Our moralistic background whispers that wild abandonment is not quite correct. Intellectually we know that we want to enjoy intercourse, that we deserve to, but we are still the bridge between our repressed forebears and our liberated grandchildren, and like it or not, that gap is gargantuan.

Often the husband is at fault, whether acknowledging this wounds his virility or not. We have been taught that it is courting disaster to criticize a man's sexual prowess for here sits his key to masculinity; so women have all too docilely taken upon themselves the blame for sex difficulties. Many men simply don't want their wives to experience orgasm for it takes the woman out of his control and into her own inner world for those few moments. She is completely transported from him and involved in her own trip.

Masters and Johnson have pointed out two of the differences between male and female orgasm: If a woman is restimulated before her orgasm drops below a plateau-phase response level, she can rapidly return to peak orgasm. In addition, a woman can maintain an orgasm for quite a long time. Neither is true for the male orgasm. So, because of this, a husband may resent his wife's orgasm and deny it to her.

Some men feel powerful only when their wives *do* achieve orgasm, and they feel inadequate if they are not able to stimulate her to that point of unrestraint. These men feel in command only when they can send a woman into ecstacy, and this sense of domination gives a heightened feeling of masculinity. But what often occurs is a deception: a woman can have intercourse with no desire at all and may pretend to reach her climax just to satisfy her mate. This is understandable if it is occasionally done as an act of giving pleasure to the man you love, but it is masochistic for a woman to constantly fake pleasure, forgoing her own gratification just to satisfy a man who won't accept the possibility of his inadequacies.

Responsible sex research is offering hope to millions of men and women who choose to utilize it. Many couples today are certainly freer about facing their problems and seeking help. However, even in our supersophisticated world, a whole range of American women are still ignorant about the basic workings of their bodies as well as the bodies of their bedmates, and yet we are urged to give full satisfaction while reaching it ourselves.

"I never even knew I had a clitoris," one woman recently admitted. "Can you imagine, over thirty years old, college educated, and I just found out it existed!" The reason this can happen is that the clitoris is often not detailed in those preteen sex manuals, especially those issued in the early 1950s.

"Didn't you masturbate as a child? Or now?" her companion asked.

"Of course not. I was always told it was dirty and would lead to dreadful things." Thanks to Portnoy's memoirs, for one, a remark like this belongs to the good old days. According to sociologist Robert R. Bell of Temple University, "Masturbation is only harmful when people suffer guilt about it. It's the guilt that's harmful." This guilt, of course, has marched down through the generations.

Many women have been told by Freudian psychiatrists that they are "frigid" because, although they enjoy vaginal intercourse, they reach orgasm only by clitoral stimulation. If we are in the midst of an orgasm cult, we are also involved in shattering the great frigidity myth. In pre-Women's Liberation days, a frigid woman was one who never experienced a vaginal orgasm. She may have experienced a clitoral orgasm, but she was labeled "frigid" if she did not climax during the act of intercourse. Under this definition, millions of women were and still are diagnosed as "frigid." More important, they believe it.

However, more and more women and medical people are abandoning the Freudian vaginal orgasm theory and accepting the fact that a strong spastic orgasm usually occurs from the stimulation of the clitoris.

Anne Koedt, one of the "Radical Women," is no longer considered so radical with her thesis "The Myth of the Vaginal Orgasm":

"Frigidity has generally been defined by men as the failure of women to have vaginal orgasms. Actually the vagina is not a highly sensitive area and is not constructed to achieve orgasm. It is the clitoris which is the center of sexual sensitivity and which is the female equivalent of the penis.

"All orgasms are extensions of sensation from this area. Since the clitoris is not necessarily stimulated sufficiently in the conventional sexual positions, we are left 'frigid.'

"What we must do is redefine our sexuality. We must discard the 'normal' concepts of sex and create new guidelines which take into account mutual sexual enjoyment."

Psychologists have broadened frigidity to include a complete disinterest in having any sexual activity, and a lack of response to sexual activity. This brings many of the "frigid" women out of the cold and into the glow of loving sex.

Better yet, Masters and Johnson would like to abolish the word *frigidity* completely. As Dr. Masters put it: "We don't know what it means. It doesn't mean anything. It means a woman who doesn't have orgasm, and it means a woman who has orgasm once a week, and her husband thinks she ought to have it twice. So we never discuss it."

And Ms. Johnson explains, "Some male who thinks of women only as sex objects must have affixed it because it is not a term that a woman would apply to a variation of her own sexual response."

In other words, what may bring you deep satisfaction during one love-making session may leave you a bit frustrated another time, since needs vary so from mood to mood and from day to day. It would be absurd, however, to state that men and women have no physiological sexual differences. As we saw in the last chapter, the clitoris is the female counterpart to the male penis. But this is not to say that it is a rudimentary penis (an inferior organ as dictated by Sigmund Freud), which inspires a surge of penis envy in a woman which she must compensate for during the rest of her life. While Freud contributed to the understanding of human subconscious and the entire field of mind probing, he limited his studies to a group of middle-class people, and then drew some conclusions which he applied to the entire female gender.

Other influential scientists have turned the tables and labeled man's envy of woman "womb envy." This does not seem any more incredible than penis envy. (To my way of thinking, man's jealousy of our ability to give birth to another human being makes more sense than our envy of a man's extra appendage.) Even one of Freud's followers, Alfred Adler, disagreed with the master's theory that women are biologically inferior, saying instead that women's "inferiority" is purely social in nature.

Today, we women are studying femininity ourselves rather than accepting the word of male "experts," and what many of us have found is that the clitoris is only the visible end of a deep sexualism within us. We have concluded that the clitoris is the only human organ designed solely for sexual pleasure.

Somehow, all this is beginning to sound like the final holocaust in the traditional battle of the sexes, with man defending his masculine caricature of aggressiveness against the shattering feminine stereotype of passivity. And the weapon being used is sex—meaningless, loveless, empty sex.

Jacqueline Onassis is quoted as saying, "There are two kinds of women; those who want power in the world and those who want power in bed"; the former refers to direct "masculine" concrete power, the latter to a more circuitous, secretive, manipulative kind of power.

But what should sex have to do with power? Is the expression of love to be used as a weapon? Certainly, it has been used by men against women for centuries, and by women (though less forcibly) against men in retaliation; and women have used it against each other in the great fight for the almighty man. We fake desire and fake satisfaction to keep our mates happy. And we are frustrated because a little gentleness, understanding, or companionship might have been all we wanted at the time. Many times when we act according to specific needs we are diagnosed as neurotic, possessive, or frigid. Our men run away, fearful that they might be losing their magic touch, and turn instead to more traditional women, in public or in private.

There will be no true sexual revolution until there is a woman's revolution. And this means shredding the cobweb of sexual myths and destroying the stereotyped roles for men and women in bed—what we need, what we should do, and how we should do it. Until this is accomplished, sex is going to become even more plastically impersonal than it is today.

We are all so alienated that there is not only a generation gap between parent and child, a sibling gap between older and younger, but a marital gap between husbands and wives. In an era when schisms are not only unnecessary but destructive, we are still perpetuating the fairy tale about woman's place in man's world. We read everything about sex in novels, learn every nuance of sexual technique from manuals, and we see it all in low-budget sex films, yet we can't make sex work for us in our own homes. Men and women, instead of turning to each other in a gesture of honesty,

wanting to give and love, or to be consoled, jump in
the hay to relieve frustrations and jump out more frustrated than ever. They turn to strangers for thrills and
sex is a dirty joke.

It is not until women are what Professor A. H.
Maslow calls "self-actualizing" people, living in and
contributing to the real world outside the four walls
of home sweet home, that they can truly give themselves in love and receive a lover's response. When we
are able to appreciate our individual abilities and personal achievements, we will also be able to put sex into
one appropriate corner of our lives; then, when the
time comes that we want to express our feelings in
physical terms, we can abandon ourselves without sham
and without shame. Whether it comes every night or
twice a month will not affect our femininity. Whether
we reach multiple orgasm or none at all does not reflect
on our sensuality. As a final result, sex may be fun
again.

Sensuality, at long last, will erupt from within us,
rather than be judged by our outer curvature. Erotic
surface beauty plays one part in our culture, but it
should not dominate the bedroom ideal. After all,
what's on the surface does fade. And if one purpose of
the feminine existence is reproduction and the second
purpose is sexual attractiveness, what happens when
both of these desert us in middle age? We become frustrated, empty, aging drudges—Tommy's doting grandmother, Jane's meddling mother-in-law, a husband's
bridge-playing, time-killing spouse.

Life does continue after fifty; we have at least
one-third of our years left, and that one-third has the

potential for far more sensuality than we knew in the immature, uninformed years. Of course, this all depends upon inner sex, and up to now, "sex" has meant primarily the outside of the female body.

9

It's What's Up Front
That Counts

"Protest the mindless boob girlie symbol of American womanhood. Help crown a live sheep Miss America. Burn bras, fashion magazines, and cosmetic goop in a freedom trash can."

That was the start of something big. Even though the lighted match never actually touched the bra (for lack of a fire permit), bra-burning has become the symbol of the Women's Liberation movement. This is partly because the communications media know it makes good copy and Bob Hope thinks it makes for good laughs. But more important, the breast has evolved into a synonym for femininity. The breast symbolizes the dual sexual and maternal role of a woman. In order for women to break down this stereotype, the bra, as a symbol of femininity, had to go.

Obviously, tossing a brassiere into a trash can does not automatically toss the breast into oblivion. Hollywood has kept the breast alive and blooming from Bow to Bardot. New York's Seventh Avenue has made the upper half of our bodies the focal point for decades, from the clinging, plunging thirties to the topless styles of today, and Madison Avenue does its part with slogans like "It's what's up front that counts" and that "Taste me, taste me" double-threat come-on.

Perhaps Norman Mailer best detailed the power of the female chest in *The Prisoner of Sex* when he described Congresswoman Bella Abzug as having "bosoms which spoke of butter, milk, carnal abundance, and the firepower of hard-prowed gunboats."

Wow! Potency like that could easily go to the feminine head.

Man has been fascinated with the female breast throughout the ages, and this captivation by one part of the opposite sex's anatomy reflects his attitude toward women in general. When his artwork portrayed Venus-type ladies, female breasts were drawn bold and brazen. During the Madonna adoration, female breasts were decorously covered up. Bosoms were bound when women wanted suffrage and equality, and they burst forth boundless when Hollywood set the sex appeal standard for our time.

Few breasts, of course, can live up to TV and movie standards, so industry has stepped forward, ever industrious, with a sizable selection of breast beautifiers which offer to fill in the empty space or take away the waste. But, not surprisingly, they often don't work out as promised, because even vitamins, hormones, and plastic surgery must ultimately bow to the self-image. After centuries of believing that a woman's main worth lies in her attractiveness, we often become unhappy, frustrated, and envious if every aspect of our appearance does not face up to current ideals. How we look upon ourselves depends upon how we've been told we should look. This is the reason why many early suffragists threw aside all their "feminine" embellishments, pulled back their hair, donned tailored suits, and shunned makeup. Only by looking like men, they believed, would women be treated the same as men and be granted previously masculine rights.

But that was long ago and far away. Today most men's wear is women's wear. No longer must we curl, tease, and spray our hair to look womanly. Where once a dress was *de rigueur,* today we can slip into pants and go just about anywhere (even Amy Vanderbilt says so).

Once we become secure enough in our femininity, we can convince men that their masculinity should not hinge upon what manner of female is clinging to his arm in a nightclub. We can adorn ourselves to whatever limit we want, for cosmetics will be adornments, not necessities.

Once we admit that we are all feminine simply by having been born female, then makeup or no, bra or braless or padded is irrelevant. In other words, pleasing a man will not make our day.

Of course, if you please your man by being yourself, that's an added bonus. But to set out each morning, lacquered and painted, cinched and penciled, is only making a thing of yourself, a thing that takes on its own materialistic importance. What happens is that you create an artificial facade and then are dedicated to preserving it for as long as you can.

On the sultriest summer day you must shield your coiffure so a chance breeze will not muss it. You turn from a kiss because it might smear your lipstick. You protect yourself against yourself as you would guard a Chippendale armchair against children's smudges.

But it is inescapable that, while furniture can be preserved indefinitely (and its value increases with age), our living bodies cannot. Time will inevitably etch scrawls that no makeup can smooth out, and desperate efforts to constantly brighten up graying hair around a lined face will at some point be futile. If our femininity depends upon attracting the opposite sex, are we feminine when we get old? Obviously not.

Let's face it. We all have our particular vanities. Aren't we still products of a feminine mystique upbringing and the masculine machismo hangover? In my own case, I have a paleness problem—if I wash my face, it disappears. That's why I grab for an eyebrow pencil each morning as soon as I've stumbled out of bed and splashed water on my face. Without that shading, I can't face the day (and the day can't face me). Lipstick, mascara, eye shadow, bra can all go. But eyebrow pencil? Never!

Life magazine once quoted an ardent young feminist who willingly gave up her short skirts and makeup, but when it came to not shaving her legs, she balked: "I'll die for the revolution, but don't ask me to not shave my legs!" Some myths seem immortal.

They aren't immortal though; myths do die. Eventually all myths are proven false simply because they are based on fancy and not fact.

Having more than my own quota of vanities, I'll confess another one here. I used to have light blonde hair which I had always felt was my physical strong point. (I haven't all that many strong points, you see, so I cherish what there is.) I was rather fond of that color and refused to face up to the eventuality that it would someday darken.

"I'll color it," I told myself, never really believing that such a day would come.

But it did. Two years ago, I had my hair cut in layers, which was a liberation, cosmetically speaking. No more hair rollers or burning electric curlers. Gone were the sticky spray can and prickly hairpins. I was free. The only problem was that my blonde hair was free too—free of me, and on the hairdresser's floor. My hair had always been lightest on the top layer, bleached by many sunny years and chlorine swims, and now this layer was one inch long. Suddenly, I was topped with a cap of dreary hair which I could identify only as dust-colored.

The strange part was that I didn't care. Although I had always dreaded the day when I would be robbed of my main physical plus, now I was facing it squarely and rather painlessly with only a bottle of highlighting shampoo in my hand.

Like most women, I still wear more makeup than just the indispensable eyebrow pencil, although I wear less and less each year. And the main reason I cut my hair short was because I liked the way it looked. I still prefer the shorter hemlines, feel happiest in clothes I look best in, enjoy the new fashions (but don't follow all of them), and am a perpetual dieter who has the disadvantage of loving to eat.

But I don't feel a slave to makeup anymore — I leave my face *au naturel* if I feel like it. I will no longer be dictated to twice a year by a misogynistic group of business people in Paris. And more important, I accept my changing features with a growing sense of resignation. I will change with age — everyone does. I will do all I can to look presentable — every man and woman should, for beauty in all its varying degrees is essential to the enjoyment of life. Women's Liberation, like all liberation, is essentially directed to that end.

One of those ever-present old sages once commented, "Women dress either for men or for other women." This means that there are two categories of women. In the first is the woman who makes herself seductive, and who therefore is an "eternal female" whose primary destiny in life is being a sexual companion. In the second category is the female who dresses for other women, and who is usually narrow-minded, catty, and frustrated, unable to "adjust" to her femininity. These two categories have been divided and subdivided until we find that ultimately, it is woman against woman in the frantic effort to catch or to keep a man.

When invited to a party, you probably wonder "What shall I wear?" followed quickly by "What will the other women be wearing?" Whether your intention is to go straight to the bait (the men) or to take the roundabout route of outdoing the other women, you will still be striving for just the right mixture of sex and class in your dress. It is an expensive, time-consuming, and emotionally wearing game. Finally, you wind up resenting any woman who looks better than you (or, even worse, who wears the same dress and looks better). Who is benefiting from all this primping and parading? Men, of course! They who set the standards are reaping the rewards.

What is completely smothered is the fun of dressing up and looking pretty. Why should we dress with a certain class of men or women in mind? For years, we have doggedly accepted any new look that's been labeled "in." We fought the midi for a while, yes, but eventually we gave in, and for this we were granted short pants to wear under the long coats. And why? Because while we are told to stay home, we are faced with actresses, novelists, and glamorous television panelists whom our husbands admire for being "feminine." So what do men want — security or seduction? Obviously both, and since it's impossible to be all things to even one man, the most sensible thing to do is to be an individual. Be yourself. Cosmetics or no cosmetics, big breasts or small, bare or booted calves— choose your own way.

One thing every woman will gain from Women's Liberation is the destruction of the youth cult. We have been cajoled into envying, worshipping, and adoring the young. Parents try to dress like their teenagers to prove there is no gap. On TV we watch the Pepsi generation romping, loving, living to the hilt, while the Schlitz set sits with a glass of foaming brew, suffering from arthritis, neuritis, and post-nasal drip. Who could help but agree that young is fun, and old is dreary — perhaps even offensive.

The result? The appalling statistic that forty percent of divorces take place after ten years of marriage. Then there is the man who turns away from the woman with whom he has shared bed and board for twenty years to marry a girl his daughter's age. Most of the time, the young girl — like the promises of TV ads for soaps and toothpastes — just does not deliver. Added to the end of a woman's childbearing days is the gnawing fear of losing the man she has served for half her life. She faces the middle of her life with trepidation.

Standards of beauty today apply only to the young. Breasts of the older woman are not erotic; lines in her face are not sensual. When we say a forty-year-old woman is beautiful, we really mean she doesn't look forty, but thirty — or better yet, twenty-five.

Standards of beauty are artificial and arbitrary. They are ideals that can never be reached. If we keep striving for them, we will lose our natural lure; our sexual appeal will hinge completely on long eyelashes, sultry lipstick, blonde hair, and a grandiose bustline. The woman who goes to the supermarket today is buying eroticism along with liquid cleaner and is bidding for hubby's attention when she adds a certain hand lotion to her grocery list.

Isn't it ironic how the ads keep shouting "Be natural!" when what they are selling is a cover-up for our naturalness? They peddle "natural" hair color because our own color is not good enough; "natural" underwear for our faulty figures; even "natural" cigarettes! An image has been manufactured which specifies which "natural" body areas are acceptable and which are taboo. Shave off underarm and leg hair and add more to the head. Flatten the tummy and lengthen the lashes. Use as many artificial accoutrements as needed to appear as "natural" as possible.

Not only is our truly natural appearance to be covered over, but our natural odor must be masked as well. In 1971, American women spent approximately $40 million to solve a "problem" they never knew existed until a few years before. Like underarm odor, vaginal smells have now been labeled "offensive," while perfumes, scented deodorants, and sachets have the desirable aromas. The solution came in the form of vaginal deodorant spray, which promises to mask unacceptable body odor with springtime freshness.

However, what the vaginal deodorant sprays deliver is not freshness but a potentially harmful chemical solution. While we spend millions of dollars trying to make ourselves more sensuous for men, we are possibly destroying our most sensual body zone. In addition, we are murdering our self-confidence by swallowing the poisonous tale that without the camouflage of these products, we are dirty and unfeminine. This, of course, is untrue, unless we agree that femininity is just another commodity that can be bought over-the-counter for a higher and higher price.

All this does not dispel beauty and sex appeal from our brave new equal world. On the contrary, they will have a larger place and a more secure position, for they will not fade with the makeup remover, nor erode with the years. One word will be added to beauty and to sex appeal, and this one word will expand and enhance the good life. The word is *human*—human beauty and human sensuality. They are more than skin deep.

10

Looking Back

"Penis envy!" men shout at us.

But not all men. There is one, Ashley Montagu, who claims "man's drive to achievement can, at least in part, be interpreted as an unconsciously motivated attempt to compensate for the lack of biological creativity."

Could the accusation of penis envy really mask the male's womb envy? Haven't you heard men boast about "giving birth" to a plan? If a man has worked on a special project, doesn't he exclaim, "That's my baby!"? As much as a man scorns any affectation which might label him effeminate—the ultimate in disdain—

isn't he prone to pride himself on being "pregnant with ideas"?

We've all heard these remarks, but the fact remains that no matter how anxious man might be to give birth in his own masculine way, he has spent his years on earth keeping down the original birth-giver. He may long have declared, "Women—we love 'em!" but he has seldom been agreeable to yielding any precious masculine space to women. He has manipulated interpretations of what is masculine and what is feminine to fit his own needs and fears—setting woman on a lofty Victorian pedestal, presenting her with equal wartime status, and pushing her three steps behind the rest of the time.

On the equality platform, women have been accepted only in dire emergencies, and even then, grudgingly. It is as Caroline Bird stated in *Born Female:* "Generally speaking, frontier conditions—wars, revolutions, and feverish boom times which provide urgent work for all hands—have motivated men and women to similar or androgynous goals. By contrast, periods of slow or orderly economic growth such as the first and fifth decades of this century have cultivated masculinity or femininity as goals in themselves. In these periods, men are encouraged to submit to industrial discipline in order to make money as the primary way to prove their 'manliness,' while women are encouraged to stay at home and be 'feminine.' "

How did man get the superior role of arranger of the sexes? How did women get a second-class role, where even the identifying word *woman* is derived from *wifeman,* the property of man?

In the last few chapters we have seen that women are born with a certain biological potential, which comprises organs, hormones, and a skeletal structure, and endows all women with inborn femininity. Men have their particular body structure, organs, and hormones too. Both sexes are also born with intellectual as well as physical promise. These mental and physical foundations, synthesized in society's molds of femininity and masculinity, are framed and formed by habits, roles, and attitudes, and should allow individuals to become sturdy structures of their sex. Obviously it doesn't always work this way, because people, unlike buildings, pulsate with emotions and feelings, and cannot stand straight and sturdy at all times.

We have learned that nature defines feminine as a biological happening. So, how did society get so influential that it could add the mythological framework to the simple original biologic basis? And how did women get slotted into a subordinate standing so long ago in human existence?

Ashley Montagu states that the divisions of labor between men and women, those time-honored male-female roles, have their origin in biological differences. But because man has always played the more aggressive part does not necessarily mean that he is "by nature" more active. What it does mean is that society has given him this part to play simply because he has not had the functions of giving birth and nursing infants. He has not been held back by maternity, so he can realize his human potential by pursuing an active life.

"It is an error," says Dr. Montagu, "to assume that the female is by nature sedentary whereas the male is by nature mobile. Such activity differences do exist between male and female, but to a large extent they would seem to be secondary differences, not primary. . . . The socially observed differences in activity between the sexes, it cannot be doubted, are to a large extent acquired rather than inherited."

Looking back on those thousands of years of history, we can see that this active-male, sedentary-female role arrangement is based on primeval conditions. The irony is that these conditions are no more, but the roles have not adjusted to any other era, including our own presumably "civilized" age of today. We are still playing parts that were applicable to the earliest people on earth, and, naive as it sounds, times have changed, and so have we, all of us, men and women, and so has the world we live in.

The rules of life were probably drawn up when the first caveman told his cavewoman: "Look, this is your home. Since you have to stay put anyway to give birth to our children, and since only you can nourish them, it makes sense to take upon yourself the job of keeping the place tidy as well. Taking care of the cave and everyone in it is a very important job since our purpose here on earth is to keep the species going. You will have to give birth to at least fifteen or twenty children, and then try to keep a couple of them alive so they can repeat the whole process.

"Now, if you do your work well, my darling, everyone will tell you how successful, wonderful, and even creative you are. And how lucky you are to have me because my job will be bringing home the food for you to cook and the animal skins for you to fashion into clothing. I will take care of you and keep our home safe."

So off he went to carry out his role, and a very demanding one it was. But in hunting for food, scrounging for shelter, defending the homestead, he was also expanding. He was learning about animals and their behavior. He was carving tools. He was meeting other precivilized men in combat and conquering them, or he was learning from defeat. He was exercising his mind in different ways every day—deciphering animal tracks, and learning about plants, weather, and weaponry. By inventing, creating, and doing, man was *becoming*.

His cavemate, meanwhile, was home, safe and snug with the cave kiddies. She was not inventing or creating, but repeating. By performing her biological functions of giving birth and nursing, she was perpetuating the species. By keeping the cave homey, gathering roots and herbs, preparing meals, she was *remaining*. While her husband was amplifying his potential, woman was encased in her biological organs, and from this primitive point on, she was considered second-rate, static, and inferior. Was she important? Sure, but only as a base for man's activities. Even in the early festivals she would join the men in celebrating *their* accomplishments and victories because *these* were the very reasons for living. There were no celebrations for a clean cave or a new baby, only for what men did to conquer nature.

From this early hunting basis, the next civilizing level was settling down on the land. It was at this agricultural time that the masculine-feminine roles were welded into historical truth. Ownership of property replaced mere survival as the purpose of life, and consequently heirs took on new importance. Earth was precious, sons were valued, and maternity was viewed as an awesome function. Just as the soil held its secrets of fertility and harvest, so women held their secrets of fertility and child-bearing. (Actually, the female part in giving birth was obvious; what was not yet understood was man's role in procreation.) So woman took her place on the first of many pedestals and around her was spun the mystique of priestess, sorceress, goddess, and Mother Earth herself.

Sounds impressive, doesn't it? Those were the days, it seems. But, looking a little closer, we see that the goddess' power was truly "out of this world." She was equated with passive waiting and unexplained mystery rather than reason or management. Anything not understood was automatically labeled "female." Men, in other words, formulated this whole feminine myth to answer their own questions about land, food, and life itself. And it worked, until they learned that womanhood was not part of growing crops and was only partly responsible for growing babies; then her pedestal was yanked away and back she went to the old washing rock.

Once these rules and roles were entrenched, everything went downhill for us girls. Mythology, law, and religion put us down as the original red-hot sinners— from the myths of Eve, Pandora, and Medea to the lofty laws of Solon, to the preachings of the Koran and the Bible, women are the baddies.

The religious pundits minced no words. In the

Koran of Islam is written, "Men are superior to women on account of the qualities in which God has given them pre-eminence."

The Orthodox Jew's morning prayer includes, "Blessed art Thou, oh Lord, our God, King of the Universe, that I was not born a woman."

In Christianity, second-classdom traces directly to Paul, who held such beliefs as, "Neither was the man created for the woman, but the woman for the man." This standard of masculine superiority was elaborated on during the papal reign of Gregory VI, when woman was ascribed to be not only man's "handmaid" but a threat to his moral salvation. And Thomas Aquinas crowned woman's reputation by portraying her as an incomplete being, an imperfect man. "It is unchangeable that woman is destined to live under man's influence and has no authority from her lord."

It is not surprising to learn of a strong reassertion of woman's dignity coming from female theologists. Elizabeth Cady Stanton, less than a century ago, undertook the writing of a "Woman's Bible," after suffering much of her life from religious discrimination. Mary Baker Eddy concentrated on studying the Bible and finally founded the Christian Science Church which portrays God as a universal father-mother. And recently, Dr. Mary Daly was quoted as suggesting, "It's time to rework the basic myths and symbols of theology in light of the new awareness of how women have been exploited."

It was not only the Judeo-Christian tradition which defiled us. Oriental ancients often burned "useless" widows on their husbands' biers; Egyptian women, though legally privileged in many ways, were socially *persona non grata*. Today, many Moslem women are still veiled and sequestered as virtual slaves.

In the agricultural age, women were property, like land and livestock. They had no rights. Women were taken from their fathers' home and tacked onto their husbands' kin. The new wife had her duties presented to her, and in turn, she delivered her children to her husband's family, along with any money or possessions she might have brought along. It's not hard to see why boy babies became favored, so much so that in certain points of history, daughters were killed at birth; the father who would agree to keep his little girl was considered very generous indeed.

These grisly traditions continued into the Middle Ages. Laws kept a woman from injury but not from a marriage she might not want or from a life of servitude she dreaded. In the days of feudalism, she was part of her husband's fief, just as the entire family was part of a suzerain. Even in the twelfth century, an age of knightly love, adoration of the Madonna, poetry, and manners, women were still forced into wedding medieval boors. One step up the status ladder, however, was now in evidence for single women; in certain areas they could own a fief, sign treaties, and decree laws. Joan of Arc, among others, proved a woman could even command troops. But these freedoms were halted at the marriage altar.

It wasn't until the Italian Renaissance that, for the first time, aristocratic women were allowed some education. From this elite group emerged powerful female sovereigns, saints, and patrons. Upper-class women were exempt from the strict morality of the times and, like Madame de Sévigné, they exercised their strength in supporting the male talent of the day; like Madame de Maintenon, they influenced the affairs of state; and, like Catherine of Siena, they demanded personal adulation.

However, while it was possible for male geniuses like Shakespeare to rise out of the masses, it was impossible for the middle- or lower-class woman to develop her potential. Not only was she refused access to education, but she was bound and gagged by traditional morality. No woman from the lower echelon could hope to escape the fireside unless, like the Sisters Brontë, she adopted a masculine name.

Across the ocean, American women had one advantage which made them more emancipated than European women—the frontier. Although customs were strictly Old World, the struggle and travail of settlement days encouraged the American gals to fight, work, and accomplish next to their men. They became everything from gunsmith to upholsterer, jailkeeper to "doctoress." When her husband died, a widow knew enough about his business to carry on. Again, as it was in the cave days, survival was the first priority on the frontier. Since women were scarce, every one of them was urged to provide an abundance of offspring so some might survive to adulthood.

Of course, women were still legal nonentities, a hangover from British common law. They were allowed no possessions, no control over their own children, no education beyond minimal reading and writing, no paying jobs except domestic servitude.

Women, like children, were to be seen and not heard; and like mental deficients, women were not allowed to vote. Women could even be beaten by their husbands, provided a stick no thicker than a man's thumb was used.

Nevertheless, these were days when the sexes were almost equal. The frontier states recognized female importance. Wyoming, Colorado, Utah, and Idaho led the rest of the country in granting suffrage to women before the turn of the century.

Then, alas, came the Machine. The hard times softened, and the spurt of energy ebbed. The Industrial Revolution arrived and equality evaporated. Once more masculinity and femininity stepped back to their respective corners. Women who wished to earn money continued doing sewing, spinning, and weaving in the home, but now they added to their day by performing the same household tasks in factories.

And as for the woman who did not have to go out to work, she was hoisted once more to the top of the stone pedestal where she was to wile away her hours as a lady of leisure (this was a very enviable state from then on). She was to become the male's ideal—soft and gentle as her lambskin powderpuff.

Ripe was the time for Women's Liberation! In the earliest Victorian days, small bands of dedicated women took up the banner for abolition and temperance, paving the way for the current campaign for sexual equality. In 1848, at Seneca Falls, New York, feminism burst forth with Elizabeth Cady Stanton's own version of the "Declaration of Independence":

"We hold these truths to be self-evident: that all

men and women are created equal; that they are endowed by their Creator with certain inalienable rights; that among these are life, liberty, and the pursuit of happiness . . . such has been the patient sufferance of the women under this government, and such is now the necessity which constrains them to demand the equal station to which they are entitled.

"The history of mankind is a history of repeated injuries and usurpations on the part of man toward woman, having in direct object the establishment of an absolute tyranny over her. To prove this, let facts be submitted to a candid world."

And "facts" of abuse were declared, including: lack of suffrage, lack of say in the laws which governed her, lack of all rights in property, including her own wages. In conclusion:

"He [man] has endeavored, in every way that he could, to destroy her confidence in her own powers, to lessen her self-respect, and to make her willing to lead a dependent and abject life."

Mrs. Stanton was to devote over fifty years to overturning these laws—eventually seeing women gain the right to control their own property and earnings, to serve as guardians of their children, to get a divorce, to sue and bear witness in court, to go to college, and to earn a living.

Betty Friedan describes a nineteenth-century woman's life as follows: "Confined to the home, a child among her children, passive, no part of her existence under her own control, a woman could only exist by pleasing man. She was wholly dependent on his protection in a world that she had no share in making:

Man's world. She could never grow up to ask the simple human questions, 'Who am I? What do I want?' "

The movement was snowballing. Amelia Bloomer in her comfortable pantaloons; Susan B. Anthony, single and persevering; the Grimké sisters; and Lucy Stone all pushed forward The Cause. Ralph Waldo Emerson and Abraham Lincoln, in the tradition of Erasmus, Moliere, and John Stuart Mill, showed sympathy for woman's lot. But handouts were still only handouts at masculine whim; the Fourteenth Amendment gave all male citizens the vote, but refused it to women.

The firing on Fort Sumter heralded the Civil War in 1861, so women were called back into society again. They were needed on the battlefields, and in schoolrooms, hospitals, and factories. When the war ended, many refused to be shunted aside. Since men were lured more by the mystique and the money of physical labor than by the gentility of school and office work, they passed over these more passive fields and left them to women. Typewriters and telephones introduced a new dimension for women workers, and during the last third of the nineteenth century, more girls than boys were graduating from high school.

Newsreel views of the suffragists of the first part of this century show them tied to the White House gates, fasting, being battered with billy clubs, parading, and demonstrating. These dramatic manifestations served to keep the issue alive while the plodders and organizers behind the scenes forced through the results. The more silent but sophisticated suffragists were playing politics. They argued that women could keep the country morally fit by means of their humanitarian causes, and soberly fit by dousing the fire water. Both methods—hard-sell and soft-sell—were important and effective, for in 1920, women finally got the vote.

What did this mean? Simply that women could vote, and they celebrated by putting Warren Harding in the White House. Discrimination was still apparent in low wages and minor jobs offered women, but the suffragist's snowball was melting. There were new causes for the social-conscious, educated women of the 1930s and 1940s—The League of Women Voters, Women's International League for Peace and Freedom, Negro rights, human rights, war victims. Feminism became a bore. One battle was over when the vote was won, but much more was needed.

Women, however, were no longer satisfied to be on that Victorian pedestal or in the latest version of the primitive cave-home. They went to college in droves, got into professions and businesses, graduate schools, and politics. They threw away their corsets, long skirts, and frills, bobbed their hair, and made sex a pleasure. They became a market for luxuries, women's novels, and magazines, and since they were working, they could afford to buy, buy, buy.

By 1940, twenty-five percent of the adult female population was working, and the war had introduced women to trucks, tractors, and cranes. Equal pay and equal standards were finally in effect, and birth control was welcomed. Then the war ended, and 300,000 women lost their jobs. American culture was at last peaceful and prosperous, so the old roles returned. Masculinity and femininity were in vogue, no matter what anyone wanted. From 1950 to 1960, women were edged out of the labor market slowly and deliberately. Women's magazine editors were now men, as were women's college professors. Many men became primary school teachers, social workers, and librarians —traditionally female occupations.

The old suffragist movement had crumbled like an antique relic, cherished by no one. Young girls heard the name Susan B. Anthony and asked "Who?" Suburbia blossomed and babies boomed. Yes, there were a few diehards around, such as the formidable Eleanor Roosevelt who joined in the demand for a sweeping constitutional amendment to guarantee women equal rights. It was Mrs. Roosevelt, in fact, who refused to let male reporters cover her press conferences, thus forcing editors to assign women reporters to the White House. Sturdy women like this kept the women's issue breathing, if not kicking.

Then, around the birth of the sixties, Esther Peterson was appointed director of the Women's Bureau under President John F. Kennedy, and she proposed a Commission on the Status of Women to eventually formulate a new policy on women. Things began rolling again. Mrs. Roosevelt's personal peeve had been an old Civil Service ruling that let officials ask for candidates of one sex or the other without giving any reason for the preference. In 1962, President Kennedy told her that he had issued the directive that women be considered for promotion in the Civil Service on an equal basis with men.

Working women were back on the upgrade. By 1966, twenty-six percent of the mothers of preschoolers were working outside the home. Women were being recognized as an essential portion of the labor force. (Today, we constitute fifty-three percent of the voting power—but are things really so different from earlier times? In our contemporary society, has our status really been altered?)

Laws change, and so must attitudes. Man is still considered to be the adventurer, hunter, and provider. He still forms the tools for survival, once a simple arrow, today a mind-boggling proton bomb. Woman once tended a dusty cave. Today she cleans her laminated home, gives birth by appointment, and disposes of her baby bottles and diapers after one using. In other words, men go out, women stay home; men *become* while women *remain*. The only difference is, our cave-living ancestors never knew any alternatives. But we do. We only have to be given the choice, ponder it, and take it.

And we are still the property of our men! As in those agricultural days of yore, we reflect our husbands' positions in the world; we are swathed in furs and jewels to show off his material accomplishments and thus his virility. Moreover, in the early 1970s, we were still legally bound to our husbands in many states; we could not freely use our maiden names even in "liberal" states like California, Illinois, Pennsylvania, and New York. In New Mexico, a widower received all his wife's "community" property, but if a man died, his wife was entitled to only half. In states like Alabama, Maine, South Dakota, Texas, and Illinois, employers were not prohibited at all from blatantly discriminating against women in areas of hiring and firing, and in training programs and promotions. The hope for remedying these legal inequities was wrapped up in the Equal Rights Amendment which was passed by Congress in March 1972 after almost fifty years of trying. But it takes more than laws to alter attitudes.

We haven't come such a long way, Baby. And why? Because our natural functions during the passage of thousands of years have been embellished with a lot of myths that are anything but natural. Nevertheless, the next thousand years will be different, a lot different.

Why should they be? you ask. If the feminist movements of the past have melted and run off in hopeless rivulets, why should this one erupt into a real revolution? Why now? Good questions. Turn to the next page and find out.

11

Why Now?

Why now? That's the kind of question that puts us on the defensive, isn't it? It implies that if the former women's movements haven't succeeded in changing the status of women significantly, why should we, in our current revolution, presume we can do what Susan Brownell Anthony and Company could not?

So, let's change the question to *Why not?* That's more positive. Now we can begin to list reasons, and there are very persuasive ones, why women are no longer accepting themselves as "deficient men," in mind or in body. We will point out why the seventies will be an era when the situations of men and women

173

will be tossed about, and out of the tumbling, tumult, and threatening will emerge an "equal" woman. Equal, I say—not identical. For we will never be men and we don't want to be. But we *will* be individuals, enjoying equality with men in opportunity and privilege.

We could say success spoiled the suffragists. Women got the vote, it's true, and that's what that movement was all about. Or was it? The suffragists believed that if women and men could both cast ballots, women would enjoy equal rights, but obviously things didn't work that way. Opportunities continued to be so disparate, in fact, that fifty years later, on August 26, 1970, millions of women emerged from their suburban homes and urban apartments and offices to demonstrate to the world that they had some unfinished business to clear up. Sure, women had the vote, but little else, because the suffragists took what they were offered and then dissolved their organization.

In *Everyone Was Brave,* William L. O'Neill points out that whenever women have organized, they have had to make sure that it was for some socially benevolent end (the early 1800s movement was ostensibly for the abolition of slavery; feminism was secondary). "Men easily came together in labor unions, trade and professional associations, and political groups which frankly appealed to the members' desire for power, profit, or protection, and no one thought the less of them for it. Women were rarely organized on such a casual basis. . . . If woman's nature was understood to be spiritual, self-denying, and supportive, then to be acceptable, her public activities had to partake of, or embody, these characteristics. But ultimately social feminism had a fatal effect on the woman's movement. . . . By driving extreme feminists underground, it prevented women from coming to grips with the conditions that made their emancipation necessary, that is, with the domestic system itself."

In other words, the feminists were just enlarging the acceptable home-and-hearth scene, and in expanding it, they were freezing the domestic *status quo*. "By stating that women ought to be liberated so they could accomplish great reform, the movement was working on the surface when the resentment was boiling underneath."

Charity volunteer work and social reform in any aspect has been traditionally a woman's second specialty (her first specialty being the immediate family). After "human rights" during the Depression and "war victims" in the forties, women found their goals in the "black movement." In the early days of President Kennedy's New Frontier, attention was directed to the South. Later it turned toward Vietnam, and finally to the movement for lasting peace. It was the women involved in these movements who decided that they were sick of doing the menial typing while the leadership was assigned to men. When the education is equal, why should women be the janitors and men the executives?

With this smoldering attitude as a backdrop, Betty Friedan came out with her study, *The Feminine Mystique*. Though other feminists had been calling out for decades, Friedan's voice was the right pitch at the right time.

Slowly women began examining the old stand-by-your-man refrain, at first within the vital social movements they still strongly supported, and later in small, intimate, consciousness-raising groups. There they rooted out their deepest personal feelings about womanhood, brought them to the surface, and tried to draw some conclusions about being a woman today.

Naturally, women have varying needs, so the moderate, politically-oriented National Organization for Women, founded by Friedan, splintered into more extreme groups. But for all women, a whole new purpose was invading life. We were facing our situation, searching inside ourselves, and ceasing to regard ourselves as some generalized, amorphous "womanhood." We were recognizing ourselves as distinct personalities.

We know that the movement called "Women's Liberation" is just a symbol of what it all means, just as Betty Friedan and Gloria Steinem are only examples of certain ideas under this umbrella term. Sceptics can laugh about the offshoots—the Radical Libs, Redstockings, WITCH, and SCUM—but they can't laugh away the whole movement because it is not aiming for "the vote" but for "the choice." Every woman, whether or not she now supports the movement, will eventually be affected by it.

Yet, some sceptics say there is no leader, no unity. Without a leader to give cohesiveness, a movement cannot succeed.

"Why not?" we reply. The women's movement may have no "leader," but it certainly has cohesiveness and is growing in unity every year. At the start of the 1970s, "Women's Lib" was a derogatory joke; one year later, many of the most conservative housewives across the country were admitting, "There might be something to this." In one year, that's a big step forward.

We may have varied aims and ideals, but when it comes to survival, we pull together. The capable woman running for office will get our support; so will the male candidate who has proven himself in favor of women's rights and issues before it becomes politically advisable. Day-care centers, abortion reform, and women's rights legislation on state and national levels will all get our backing. Unlike the seventy-two-year-old suffragist movement, the current movement will not narrow its aims for one golden goal, but will embrace an immense project—Equality. We will not be satisfied with a token handout, but will demand equality in the whole spectrum of life.

The "new feminism" of this century is based on a very primary platform. It does not have the more superficial goals of suffrage and social reform. We are striking deeply into the very foundations of our way of life. With new insights illuminated by women like Betty Friedan, Simone de Beauvoir, Kate Millett, and Germaine Greer tucked under our arm—insights that are relevant today—we are knocking down one side of the Establishment, while other minorities are striking at the opposite side. What must come out of this attack, of course, is the collapse of traditional power platforms and their power moralities. Women are objecting today to the parade of breasts and buttocks in Atlantic City; girls are rebelling alongside, not behind, the young men on campuses. No longer content with sandwich-making, we demand to be in on the decision-making.

This brings us to the first of two pervading move-ments in our country which are helping the develop-ment and success of Women's Liberation: The demand for universal equality. The current period of the twen-tieth century is the Age of Minorities—young people, blacks, Indians, ethnic groups, and females.

Many sociologists have pointed out the similarities between society's treatment of blacks and of women (we should now add browns and Indians, as well). First, says society, members of these groups are graced with inferior intelligence. In addition, they possess a primitive emotional nature and sensuality. They are all content with the way things are (and this satisfac-tion, say men, is proof that women's lot must be the best of all possible lots).

Like blacks, browns, and reds, women survive in the white male's world by utilizing several wily and deceitful tactics, such as an ingratiating manner to please the "lord and master." (This works in charm-ing a traffic patrolman out of a traffic ticket or seducing a boss into a pay raise.) And if that fails, we women assume an air of helplessness and inexperience.

It's frightening how ingrained these habits are. While writing this book, I was thoroughly immersed in Women's Liberation, its aims, goals, and beliefs, its detractors, and its potentials. Yet, I found myself re-sorting to what I thought was forever banished from my consciousness—feminine helplessness.

Last winter I bought a carpet from a small sub-urban store. To have it placed in my car, I drove be-hind the shop into a rather narrow alley where another car was already parked. I made it in easily enough. But after the car was loaded, I realized I would have to back out, and since the car was just a few months old, without thinking I turned to one of the nearby workmen and asked if he would back it out for me (don't we all know that men are better drivers?). Of course, as soon as I asked, I could have bitten off my tongue. I was struck by the reflexiveness of this feminine wile, how second-nature it was.

Helplessness is acceptable when one is untrained for some performance, like brain surgery or tree pruning. But I was certainly accomplished enough as a driver to back out a car—at least the odds were with me. It was just a subconscious habit, a latent cavewoman hangover, that sparked forth and urged me to ask a man to do it for me.

What finally happened was ironic. As it turned out, none of the workmen could drive a stick-shift. So, saved by the shift, I slid behind the wheel and maneuvered the car (rather aptly, I thought) back through the alley, between the parked car and wall, and into the street beyond. God in *Her* heaven, I joked, had come to my rescue!

The tactic of helplessness is embraced by the minorities and what it accomplishes is a boosting of the masculine mystique. It has made us depend upon men to get us out of tight spots. But helplessness is outmoded—it is an embarrassment in today's specialty world. Most housewives will admit that they have been forced to move into the male fields of electrical and mechanical repair. When a man is out of the house breadwinning most of the day, his wife copes with the problems of running her instrument-filled household.

At least up to the point where the problem must be passed on to an expert.

Today, minor fixings are up to the Mrs.; major repairs are up to the specialist—plumber, electrician, or carpenter. And why *should* husbands (as part of their masculine burden) be "born Mr. Fixits"? One can't be an expert in everything. In this complicated age, why not give specific problems to the specialists and leave both men and women free to pursue their own specialties?

Let's not "liberate" ourselves into the roles of men. What we want to do is redefine sex roles, those traditionally masculine and feminine parts, so that we will all have a chance to become exciting, stimulating, accomplishing individuals.

If a minority is to gain power, it needs to identify its past and its traditions and establish its historical importance. Then it can better identify and strengthen its goals for the future. Like Indians, blacks, and the other ethnic groups, we women are pulling together our culture and background in a search for uniqueness and unity. We have gathered a voluminous amount of written material, from profound theses to gut handbooks and pamphlets. We even have a theater group producing feminist plays.

Unfortunately, it has long been assumed that because women are missing from our history books, they were inconspicuous and unimportant in the growth of America. Predominantly male historians and textbook writers have emphasized the role of Roger Williams as a religious heretic, but have ignored Anne Hutchinson, just as forceful a heretic. They have illuminated the names of John Adams and Paul Revere, but we don't read much of Mercy Otis Warren, not only one of the first American playwrights but an early instigator of the Revolutionary War and a leader of the Anti-Federalist forces who demanded that a Bill of Rights be added to the Constitution.

How many students know that the first American poet was a woman, Anne Bradstreet, or that the second American to win the Nobel Peace Prize was Jane Addams?

Today, textbooks are being written by women and men who acknowledge the fact that there were some women who influenced our cultural heritage. This outpouring of information is helping to weave a tapestry of tradition which cannot help but bring us together with pride and purpose.

We have gone full cycle from that time when, because of a purely biological basis, we began our male-dictated style of living, to now, when our maternal function is waning. We have come to the second problem of our times which is helping Women's Liberation—the population explosion. Solving this problem means putting an end to the primary purpose women have embraced throughout the history of civilization.

Once, procreating was a vital necessity if the human race was to remain in existence. In those days, giving birth was perilous, and it was unusual that a child reached adulthood. Nursing a child was a hindrance to mobility. Today, giving birth not only is unnecessary but is, in fact, getting to be a "no-no."

"Our bodies," says Lisa Hobbs in *Love and Lib-*

eration, "are now obsolete in an over-populated world."

Remember, ten years ago, when your older sister breathlessly announced that she was going to have a baby, and everyone's first reaction was, "Oh, how wonderful!" followed by congratulatory cards, baby-showers, and lots of advice?

Today, if your younger sister were to reveal the same coming event, the response would likely be a lackadaisical, "Was it an accident?" Your daughter may face open scorn and disappointment; your grand-daughter, possibly, will be forced to apply for a birth license or to pay a fine. This certainly dashes a splash of icy water on that "boy for me and a girl for you" idea, doesn't it? Especially when we have been instructed for centuries on the worthiness of birth-giving. Prestige in the seventies belongs to the sterile—the man who has undergone a voluntary vasectomy or the woman who voluntarily makes sure she cannot "have accidents."

However barren and romanceless as population control may appear, the prospect of *no* control is purely horrific. We have all been exposed to the frightful pictures of the over-population problems right now. One-third of the world's people are going hungry; by the end of the century, that number will be multiplied many times.

The emergency of a crowded world has been plunked before us. Each year over 100,000 American men assume their role in contraception through voluntary sterilization. Birth control, once denounced by "liberals" as "racial suicide," is now accepted by members of virtually every religious group (regardless of what their leaders preach). Abortion, once the foulest word in the dictionary, has been forced upon legislators as a situation that must be worked out. Just a few years ago, an abortion was permissible, when allowed at all, only to save a mother's life; today, it is also permitted in many states when a woman's mental and emotional well-being are at stake. In 1971, four states, Alaska, Hawaii, Washington, and New York, were performing abortions virtually on demand.

Meanwhile, abortion opponents raise their strident and desperate cry: "Liberalizing abortion laws will lead to promiscuity and murder of the elderly!"

Others, like the state senator who claimed that a woman "has numerous emotional highs and lows" during pregnancy and she might succumb to one of these "low" moments if the abortion law of his state were to be liberalized, intimate that women will claim rape or incest (where applicable) just to avoid the "inconvenience" of another child.

How unsophisticated men like this are concerning women. How pompously they moralize for us, regarding us as mindlessly sensual and immoral, needing reasonable male legislators to set us straight. And these are men who claim to "cherish womanhood." What they really cherish is the immortality of their sperm.

They don't grasp this important fact: the decision to undergo an abortion is one of the most traumatic decisions a woman will ever have to make. What they don't empathize with is the depth of the woman's agony. Most of the time, the case against having that child is so overwhelming that there is no other choice for the mother to make. She may be destitute; she might have been raped; she might be a middle-class girl in love with her boyfriend; she might be a housewife who took potentially harmful drugs before knowing she was pregnant and finds the odds are against her having a normal child. Or, she may be a woman who simply does not want to be a mother.

It is possible to be ready for sex and/or love, but not ready for parenthood—men know that very well. A woman today deserves the right to make that choice. Pregnancy can be ecstatic when a woman wants that child, but an absolute horror when she does not. And in such cases, the child all too often ends up as a "battered child."

What the abortion opponents don't accept is the fact that once the choice is made, legally or not, it will be carried out. A woman desperate enough to want an abortion will get it—somehow. As Shirley Chisholm points out in her autobiography, *Unbought and Unbossed,* "Experience shows that pregnant women who feel they have compelling reasons for not having a baby, or another baby, will break the law, and even worse, risk injury and death if they must to get one."

The problem now comes down to who will do it and how much will it cost. If the woman is wealthy, the problem is easily solved—she can fly to one of the states where the operation is legal, just as her older sister may have flown to London or Sweden. If she is poor, the agony of making the decision is multiplied by the problem of where to get the money. If she cannot get the money, she resorts to the advice of friends and tries anything from acid douches to wire coathangers. The result all too often is that she is maimed, becomes sterile, contracts some disease, or dies. In addition, she is labeled a criminal and possibly prosecuted, as was young Shirley Wheeler in Florida. Ms. Wheeler was sentenced to two years on probation in 1971 for undergoing an abortion, tantamount to manslaughter in her home state.

It is women who are poor that the unfair abortion laws are punishing. These laws are basically puritanical punishment for enjoying sex and then seeking to undo that resulting penalty, pregnancy. When a woman decides upon an abortion in most states, she is forced to plead her case before a panel of arbitrating psychiatrists, pay an exorbitant physician's fee, or, if she cannot afford this, she is propelled into the unskilled, unsanitary hands of the "woman-handlers."

By liberalizing the abortion laws we will save the lives of people who are desperate enough to go ahead with their abortions no matter how despicable the circumstances. And the public is beginning to understand this. In 1967, a Gallup poll showed that twenty-one percent of women felt abortions should be available to anyone who wanted one. Two years later, this percentage had risen. Today, even many Roman Catholics feel the issue should be one of individual conscience rather than theological statute.

Pro-abortion or not, our prime concern—pro-creation—is being erased from our lives. What will happen to us if we have nothing else to take its place? We will have to be adequately self-equipped so that we will not have to bear a child to feel fulfilled. That is not to say that giving birth will be completely obliterated, but in the brave new world of over-population, it will become a privilege not to be abused. We are going to have to prepare ourselves and our daughters for this new world.

Catherine Drinker Bowen wrote, "Perhaps the real turn in the road will come—and I predict it is coming soon—when more than two children in a family will seem bad taste, like wearing mink in a starving village. No woman can devote a life to the rearing of two; she cannot even make a pretense of it. When the mother image loses its sanctity, something will take its place on the altar. And any writer knows that when the image of the heroine changes, the plot changes with her. Such an event could alter, for both men and women, the whole picture of American life."

If more women will be working outside the home, as the trend seems to be, one more problem that will have to be acted upon is child-care centers.

Day care—what does it mean to working women? Take Martha's case: at 8:00 A.M. every weekday, this factory worker drops her three-year-old daughter at the door of the company nursery before running on to work. Day care, to Martha, means being off welfare.

Her boss's wife, Alice, does basically the same thing. She leaves her young son at a private school across town. Day care to Alice means continuing a career she doesn't need financially, but one she has spent twenty years educating herself for. Her career is something she is adding to her marriage, not giving up, and day care lets her do this.

For many other women, however, day care signifies no care. Just bring up that topic of day-care centers and a shiver of distrust runs through them. They conjure up a picture of somber, silent infants lying in rows of cribs, watched over by unloving, sterile caretakers.

In 1971, 12.5 million children under fourteen years of age had mothers who worked. For children like these, supervision is essential, either private, or public. And this is not a new problem. During the Civil War, a center was opened in Philadelphia for those children whose mothers were sewing bandages for the Union Army. In the 1930s, the WPA opened centers to provide jobs for teachers and nurses while educating poor children. Federal funds were allocated to nursery schools during World War II when mothers had to work in munitions plants. The funds were withdrawn after the war's end so that women would have to go back home and yield their jobs to the returning soldiers. In other words, day-care supervision is fine if an emergency exists, but it becomes "unnatural" in peacetime.

Today things are changing. An emergency does exist for both working mothers and full-time housewives. Many women would not be able to work if they did not have a free nursery for their children. Most working women do not qualify for baby-sitting deductions; they work for minuscule pay and often lose money by working. If a mother must resort to less-than-the-best in day-care facilities for her child because of financial reasons, then the child is the loser—and ultimately, America is the loser.

What *is* the best day-care situation for a child? First, the facilities must not be crowded (five children to one teacher says the federal government, but many fine private schools have a greater ratio than this). There must be a wealth of appropriate educational material for children of all age levels. Strict nutritional and health requirements are a must. But what parents fear most is that their child will not get enough old-fashioned "tender loving care." They fear that the atmosphere of a day-care center is too impersonal. A caring atmosphere is vital, they feel, and they're right.

According to *Newsweek*, Professor Jerome Kagen of Harvard, a participant in the White House Conference on Children, commented, "The only thing that's important is the psychological quality of the child's experience." A youngster needs standards of success which he can follow and to set these up, "we just need humanitarians—beautiful people."

But can anyone be as "beautiful" as mother? At the risk of sounding heretical, *yes*. There have been numerous studies made in an attempt to prove that placing children in day-care centers is harmful, but none have succeeded. Why? Because, while a mother has a very special place in the life of her child, there comes a point when other adults are needed, as well as the stimulation of other children. A homey atmosphere can be combined with learning and playing in a good school. By means of scheduled teaching and recreation, a child may feel he is progressing with his peers.

No mother, no matter how dedicated, can devote her entire thinking day to her child. Most of the time, she is trying to keep him occupied and out of her hair so she can get other things done. Not because she doesn't love her child. But after all, she is an adult with a grown-up mind which cannot expand while restricted to the company of a three-year-old—from his first glass of juice in the morning to his last drink of water at bedtime.

According to *McCalls* magazine "a recent study showed that a full-time homemaker spends relatively little time in interaction with her children—less, in fact, than two hours a day, excluding the time she spends with them while she attends to other household duties. Employed women spend only forty-two minutes less time with their children than full-time home-makers!"

Which brings us to the mother with a career, like Alice, who is working solely for the thrill of her job. Domesticity is no longer the whole feminine role for growing numbers of women. Over half a million of their children are in licensed day-care centers. What happens to the rest? Many more thousands are in un-licensed facilities, and the greatest number of all are still cared for at home by baby-sitters or relatives. All that most of this latter group can hope for in the way of mental stimulation is that the TV set is working and "Sesame Street" is on.

Yet, what Alice wants for her son is no different than what Martha wants for her daughter—the best. The difference is that Alice can pay for excellence and Martha cannot, so she needs help. Since our country will benefit from Martha's daughter as well as from Alice's little boy, we should provide that help.

Now we get to the "everyday housewife" who doesn't want to go out to work but who could use a little free time for herself. If community day-care centers were as available as parks and libraries, a mother could leave her children there for a few hours while she relaxed by shopping, reading, or resting. Or she could be at home taking care of a child who might be ill. Or she could recuperate from the latest bug. You might have a mental image here of a cluster of mothers wantonly abandoning their children and dashing off to endless rounds of cocktail lunches, but this is rather extreme.

If you were asked to give criteria for the sort of day-care center you would want for your community, one that you would not hesitate to leave your child in, you would probably come very close to the federal day-care facilities standards. And if you saw your child playing happily in such a center, you would feel no pangs of guilt about wanting a few hours alone—right?

Now, why should these standards remain so debatable? For welfare mothers, day care is an economic necessity; for working mothers, it is at least a practical need; and for career-girls-by-choice, it is a personal need. Community, industry, and government must work together in financing and establishing adequate child-care facilities so that they are available to every mother and each child. Surely a country wealthy enough to send a series of men to the moon can provide day-care opportunities for our children.

Women's Liberation is working for the elimination of barriers put in the way of not only the career woman but the housewife who is faced with supporting her family or who wants to pursue her own development. So, if a woman's place is not necessarily only in the home, where then is it?

12

A Woman's Place
Is Where She Wants It

Not so long ago, a TV reporter, chatting with some children, asked one little boy, "What would you like to be when you grow up?"

"A doctor," the boy replied.

The reporter then turned to a nearby girl. "And what about you, honey?" he offered. "Would you like to be his nurse?"

That, ladies, is how we begin to slip into our woman's-place-is-in-the-home stocking. We women are possibly the greatest discriminators against ourselves, with the backing of society all the way.

Early in the seventies, the *New York Times* ran a

story about job bias against women, quoting Catherine East of the Labor Department as saying, "Psychologically it's easier for a woman to cop out than a man to give up and quit. . . . Society will say a woman's doing the right thing when she quits."

A worker at General Motors reinforced this observation by pointing out, "Our women never went into skilled trades programs—they seemed to be afraid to even try."

A worker at Ford, however, projected a sliver of hope for the future, remarking, "The younger women are more pushy. They sign up for the better jobs. If the foreman says anything about it, they'll look at him like he's crazy."

Her coworker agreed. "These younger women will not take what the older women will take."

But how does this apply to you, a housewife and mother? A wide range of literature is available for and about the professional career woman. In this book, we are interested in the professional homemaker, or that growing new breed, the combination of career woman and homemaker.

Like everyone else in this precarious world, even the professional homemaker can lose her job. What would happen to you and your family if your husband were to die? Or you got a divorce? What if your income should plummet and you were to find yourself in real economic straits? Suddenly the outside world and what it can offer you are very important.

Equal opportunities become relevant when you are concerned about making as much money as you can and getting the job you are capable of performing.

If you are a strapping young woman you might want that job lifting supermarket crates because it offers a higher salary than clerking the check-out counter. If you have sold cosmetics door-to-door for ten years in your neighborhood, you might want to branch out into selling insurance, and you won't accept some drivel about insurance not being "a woman's game." Suddenly, milady, you want those employment doors swung wide open for you, and no fair slamming them shut just because of the biological fact that you can give birth to children.

So, if you will just bear with me while we delve a bit into some facts and figures (tedious, yes, but very revealing), we can take a look at the job situation, which right now is not so hot for you as a female. Let's see why, and what's being done about it.

Since our primary location has been the home, we women have been generally unambitious and lackadaisical about demanding rights in the marketplace. We've let ourselves be convinced that it's tough out there in the man's world—too rough for a woman. Take Aunt May, who began working as a telephone operator when her youngest child turned six. She placed herself snugly in the hands of the phone company: Her employers planned her working hours to encompass any five days of the week, day or night, with holidays thrown in at the convenience of Ma Bell. They still call her in an emergency, knowing that unless Aunt May is literally paralyzed with illness, she can be counted on to get to work. And yet, for all this she is thankful.

"This year I got Christmas Eve and Presidents'

Day off," she announced one time, glowing with gratitude.

Aunt May is certain that the telephone company is doing her a favor by paying her to work in the outside world. She has been conditioned to believe her only worth is in the home, and she can't quite understand why this great organization actually needs her services. So she takes the work week they assign her and the low-status job; she accepts the morning emergency calls to work and the holidays spent on the switchboard. Give up her job? Never. Just having it is her *raison d'être*.

Discrimination seems almost too mild an epithet here—bigotry, injustice, even blatant unfairness express it more exactly. Yet, because we are the "gentle sex," let's settle for *discrimination*. It's a nice bland word. *Bigotry* belongs to the militant.

For the housewife, unskilled and untrained, the labor market can be a slave market. As with Aunt May, it can take you in, wring you of energy, and grant you a fraction of the salary a man is getting for the same (or equivalent) job and even less of his pension. As a telephone operator, Aunt May holds, according to the Equal Employment Opportunity Commission (EEOC), the "least desirable major job in the system in terms of both pay and working conditions" with almost no room for advancement, "virtually intolerable" working conditions, and an astronomical turnover rate. "Telephone operator" is almost exclusively a woman's job, as are low-level clerical jobs and the lowest-level management positions.

It's not hard to understand why the EEOC

labeled the Bell System "without doubt, the largest oppressor of women in the United States." However, Bell is not the only oppressor. Despite Title VII of the Civil Rights Act, "protective" laws, obligatory maternity leaves, unequal retirement laws, and benefit inequities all exist today.

A woman may be able to make a place for herself where she wants to, but she has to work twice as hard as a man to get it. The unemployment rosters reflect her situation: in 1968, 4.8 percent of women were unemployed against 2.9 percent of men. When the EEOC began investigating sex-discrimination charges, one of the first batches came from female factory workers claiming they were customarily laid off before the men.

We are the most dispensable group of working people. "Like blacks and the very young," wrote Alice Rossi in *Atlantic,* "[women] have traditionally been the expendable portion of the labor force which employers have been free to woo or reject in accordance with fluctuations in production, sales, patient, client, or student load. Only 40 percent of employed women work full-time all year; 32 percent work full-time part of the year, and 20 percent work part-time for part of the year. As a result, most employed women do not build up seniority in their jobs, and it is far easier for employers simply not to hire additional workers than to fire long-standing employees."

As far as salary is concerned, many employers admit that, yes, they offer us less pay. Why? Because we accept less!

In 1972, women were averaging 59 percent of a

man's pay (no step upward, for in 1955, our earning power was 64 percent of a man's salary). The median earning for a male was over $8,000 a year, and for a female, under $5,000. Thirty-two million women are now working for reasons which vary from voluntary desire to support of dependents. Salary-wise it does not really pay for these women to go to college. Even with advanced education, a woman brings home about seventy cents to a man's dollar. And if she has a degree, or graduate credits, her average wage doesn't improve at all.

Discrimination is used by employers, labor unions, and employment agencies against us. And many states offer no protection for women against unfair job practices. What they do offer is a batch of "protective" labor laws which provide for regulations for health and safety on the job and at the same time make it difficult for many women to work where they want and where they might both contribute and benefit.

One young college girl, for example, was refused a summer job by an employer who explained, "We don't have a rest room for women, and no rest room, no women. State law says that. Sorry."

Individual state labor laws like this one also set limits on lifting weights and on working hours, which would be fine if the laws applied to men as well as to women. As Governor Rockefeller of New York once claimed, we need laws to protect "working people" rather than just working women. Women are legally considered too fragile to work overtime, but how many housewives do you know who stop working after eight hours, and who don't iron, wash clothes, or go out for groceries after dark? Utah sets the limit for lifting at thirty pounds and carrying at fifteen pounds; isn't this lightweight compared to carrying your forty-pound child to bed, or lugging around a twenty-five pound prewalker?

Other states prohibit women from holding what they consider "unsuitable" jobs, for example, mixing, selling, or dispensing alcoholic beverages, although women can work in a bar as a cocktail waitress (naturally, a waitress' salary is nowhere near a bartender's). In Missouri, a woman cannot work around moving machinery, but no one cares what she does at home with an electric knife, a vacuum cleaner with its myriad attachments, or a rotary lawn mower. Sounds like these laws are protecting male bartenders and machinists rather than women, doesn't it?

These laws are not only antiquated but illegal. Title VII *prohibits* discrimination because of race, color, religion, national origin, or sex, in hiring, upgrading, and all other conditions of employment. "Unsuitable" jobs, says this law, refers only to those jobs restricted by "community" standards of morality or propriety (such as rest room attendant). The other restrictions allowed are for reasons of authenticity, like modeling, or jobs in the entertainment industry, where sex applies as an essential qualification.

The government has stated that these so-called state protection laws "although originally promulgated for the purpose of protecting females, have ceased to be relevant to our technology or to the expanding role of the female worker in our economy."

However, only a federal constitutional amendment can equalize the legal status of men and women. Without this, we are still at the mercy of these individual state laws and the legislators who write and pass them. The federal government has begun applying pressure against some obviously discriminatory practices. For example, they have threatened to withhold federal contracts to any university which is not giving its women a fair share. Also, the Supreme Court has ruled that an employer cannot exclude a woman from a job because she has children at home, unless he excludes a man for the same reason. Later, the Court ruled that men may no longer be given preference over women in administering estates. The EEOC receives and investigates charges like these, and from there, the Attorney General or the Justice Department steps in to remedy wrongs. But these remedies grow out of our complaints: No gripes, no rights.

Now, you may ask how practices like these could have arisen. What about that Bill of Rights? Doesn't it apply to women?

The Constitution mentions our rights in the Nineteenth Amendment, which gives us the vote; we are also allowed to run for the Presidency—legally. But as far as the Constitution goes, the "rights of man," alas, means just that.

Equal protection under the law, the right to use our own name, the right to own a business, the right to make contracts, the right to domicile—all these rights are dependent upon the whims of state legislatures. Only through the Equal Rights Amendment will we have a national commitment to end legal sex discrimination. Once it is ratified, we can end, as well, time-consuming bickering, registering of complaints, and plodding through months of court procedures which often take the starch out of one's determination to equalize woman's situation.

Here, again, we must put the blame for job discrimination upon those old myths (adding some younger ones born for the occasion). Myths like:

1. Women don't have to work!

Most of the 40 percent of our American work force which is female would cry "False!" They are largely in the labor market to support themselves and their dependents. More than one out of every ten families is headed by a woman; 20 percent of full-time working women do not earn over $3,000 a year; 40 percent earn between $3,000 and $5,000 annually.

Women, like men, work because of that stark word, *need*: a need for food and shelter. I do not even attempt to discuss in this short space the other "needs" of women—to contribute to the outside world, to put children through college, to buy kids those special luxuries like ballet lessons or a Cub Scout uniform, or the extra money which is never really "extra."

2. Women work only to get a husband.

If you consider that 60 percent of all women workers are married, that 38 percent have children under eighteen years of age, and over four million have kids under six; and if you realize that almost half of all women over sixteen years of age are working, and that over half the women of childbearing age work, then you will also realize that getting a husband is a motive for only a small number of working women.

3. Women have a higher absentee rate than men.

Actually, men lose more days from work a year because of disability than women do, including days lost for pregnancy and childbirth. So that shoots that argument.

4. Women show a higher turnover rate than men.

Wrong again. According to the Bureau of Labor Statistics, turnover rates depend mainly on the nature of the job. In the low-skilled and clerical jobs, men quit as often as women. In the fields requiring skill and having more stimulating work, men and women both are reluctant to quit.

5. Women are well off the way they are (or, women control the wealth of this country).

This might be true if you define controlling the wealth of this country as controlling the weekly grocery list. When less than 3 percent of the working women compared with 28 percent of men make over $10,000 a year, one can hardly say women control wealth. A minority of women own stocks listed on the major exchanges. In many cases this represents stocks listed under wives' names for tax purposes. And we all know how much control women have over the decisions made by the large and powerful companies—none. In other words, any housewife will admit that striving to stay within a budget today does not constitute controlling the wealth of these United States.

6. Women are "different," so they must be treated "differently."

Here is probably the root of this particular evil—discrimination. Treated "differently" automatically means treated "inferiorly." First, that old menstrual bugaboo is held aloft as a reason for low job performance. Aside from the fact that very few women are seriously bedded down with a bad period, medicine has advanced enough, especially through hormone therapy, to help even the most afflicted woman with menstrual or menopausal problems.

Second, inferior treatment equals menial jobs because, it is said, women are better at "detail work." The "detail work" we are supposedly so talented in is limited, however, to the stringing-beads category: "Detail work" in cardiovascular surgery is suddenly not our bag and men take over there.

The "detail work" myth strikes hardest at women with science backgrounds. Their employers often take advantage of their great desire to work and hand them chores as lab assistants, while men with lesser qualifications often gain the more rewarding research work.

The facts of job life say that women should be delegated "traditional" duties. For example, though graduating with a university degree, the Ms. will probably be settled behind a desk to file, type, and speed-write, while her male classmate will get steered into executive training. Or, she will teach fifth grade indefinitely while a Mr. looks forward to a principal's post.

Selling behind a counter is another area of glaring prejudice, where better-educated women often make as little as 40 percent of a man's pay. How many furniture saleswomen have you seen? Too much commission involved here, so it's a male-dominated department.

All this adds up to: Need a job? Learn to type.

Put another way: No matter what you've studied, from anthropology to zoology, the typewriter holds the key.

Or *held* the key, for now women are speaking up in protest. In the area of hiring practices alone, women are complaining four to one over men to the EEOC, and the Labor Department is up to its ears trying to sort out complaints and program ways to act on them. This means that eventually a woman will be able to step into society's swing before, during, or after marriage—if she wants to, if she has to, and if she is capable. Which is, after all, exactly what we're asking.

Isn't it amazing that we are not too "different," too "emotional," or too "frivolous" for the daily life-and-death decisions concerning home and family? We are responsible enough to be depended upon to feed our families the finest foods and to provide comfortable shelter; we are reliable enough to nurse sick sons and daughters—and even husbands who are down with the flu. But when it comes to dollars and cents, the politics of running the world, then all our "inferior" characteristics are cited to our disadvantage. Suddenly the doors close.

Today, we constitute a grand total of 11 percent of the professional world: 7 percent of the doctors, 3 percent of the lawyers, and in the engineering game, 1 percent is female. Kind of poor representation, isn't it? It is up to us to redefine our roles so that home-family-career can be one continuous process. At the very least, we should be prepared enough and accepted enough to get an adequate job if our economic situation demands it.

In the area of politics, stateswomen like Shirley Chisholm, Bella Abzug, and Martha Griffiths are urging women to get away from manning telephones and stuffing envelopes and get into the Senate and the House of Representatives. One way women can start preparing for political life is through involvement in the National Women's Political Caucus formed in 1971. The aims of this group include reforming the party structure to assure all women an equal voice in decision making and in selection of federal, state, county, and precinct candidates.

Politics, up to now, has been largely a male-dominated arena. In 1971, there were only Margaret Chase Smith in the Senate and a dozen women in the House. There were no female Cabinet members, nor women governors, nor women mayors of major cities.

"Does this really matter?" you might ask.

Absolutely, because women have shown a tendency to give priority to humane answers to issues, rather than to politically expedient ones—not because we are morally superior to men, but because we have been less corrupted by society and politics. Part of the masculine mystique is nourished by waging wars and bloody battles—femininity shuns this. The polls of the past years have indicated that women are sympathetic toward peace moratoriums and marches, and toward domestic spending; their husbands are prone to pull the lever for heavy military expenditures.

Yet, if no women are in our government, who is going to make our views mean something? In fact, who will even care, unless we exercise some political clout? It's clear that men do not care; they're content, on the

204 / A HOUSEWIFE'S GUIDE TO WOMEN'S LIBERATION

whole, to keep us in the hole. It's up to us to put ourselves in the forefront, if not personally, then by supporting capable candidates. Our power may be behind the throne today, but tomorrow let's move around in front. Let's get into some of those offices, legalizing this potency we are supposed to have.

In our "traditional" job area of education, nine out of ten elementary teachers are women, while the superior position of principal is held by men, eight times out of ten. On the higher levels of education, women constitute 46 percent of high school teachers and 22 percent of college teachers. Here, in the university world, sex discrimination is so rampant that, in 1969, the Department of Health, Education and Welfare undertook an investigation which culminated in such actions as freezing $400,000 in federal aid to the University of Michigan until its unfair practices were rectified, and threatening the University of Pittsburgh with cancellation of federal funds. At the Ivy League University of Pennsylvania, women faculty members were treated unfairly in days worked, in rank (women were junior assistants while men rose to associate level), and in salary (which ran 10 percent below men's).

We have steadily lost ground in the education field since the 1920s. Teaching is no longer something a woman can "always fall back on" when her children start school or move away. Which proves again that the longer we neglect women's employment rights, the harder it will be to find work if the need is suddenly thrust upon us. Even the fail-safe area of teaching no longer guarantees a livelihood.

In medicine, we are ignoring an entire class of individuals that could help fill a need that grows more desperate every year. Against the woman who wants to be a doctor society has built unreasonable blockades, the greatest apparently being reconciling family life with a medical career.

A female doctor is still considered to be a female before being a human being and a doctor. She is supposed to give up having a family if she is so foolhardy as to pursue a medical career. Dr. Leona Baumgartner, former New York City Commissioner of Health, was quoted in *Medical World News*: "What women in medicine ought to say is, 'Now, look. Make it possible for us to have our families and do our jobs too.' "

The way things are now, many women doctors just drop out because of a lack of day-care facilities or domestic help. Others plot their pregnancies to fit into brief vacation periods. An intern and resident physician often works a ninety-hour week. It is unrealistic to expect a woman intern to have her baby during a two-week vacation and then go back to work without some detriment to her mental and physical health. Despite this, Dr. Baumgartner states that 84 percent of women students finish medical school as compared to 91 percent of men, a difference of minor significance.

One proposal that has been made is to let women doctors work shifts of eight hours so that the other two-thirds of the day can be devoted to themselves and their families. Some hospitals are exploring two-year internships for married women physicians so they can work shorter hours over a longer period of time.

The next question is why hasn't this been done

before, in light of the ever-growing gap in the patient-physician ratio? A possible answer is the male power structure of the medical establishment. Medical schools and training hospitals are geared to single male students. Women doctors, married male interns, and residents are all discriminated against.

The next statement should be a demand: We must utilize womanpower in the field of medicine if we want to have healthy people. The proportion of female doctors in the United States is so abysmally low that only South Vietnam, Madagascar, and Spain have a lower proportion—rather deplorable for the "leading nation" in the world.

It is all too easy for us, the housewives and the at-home workers, to shrug and say, "Too bad things are so rough for career girls. Sure they should have the right to earn equal pay for equal work, and they should be allowed the same opportunities to enjoy self-growth, and we should utilize their talents in fields we so desperately need them in . . ." Etcetera, etcetera.

But do you realize how we say "they" and "them," never "we" and "us"? We at-homers are often quick to recognize inequities but pass them off as irrelevant to us. "It's too bad," we say in essence, "but we have our own problems at home. Let *them* fight for equal pay."

It's understandable, but regrettable, because when the need for more income does arise for you and me, the situation suddenly becomes deplorable. It's only when we are left to support ourselves and our families that we know the powerlessness and frustration aroused by discrimination. Once we need the money to live, we *want* it; and when we are faced with menial, low-paying work when we could do more, we become embittered and depressed.

The answer is not easy. It goes beyond government laws and state reforms, as necessary as these are. It means digging right down until we hit the root of the problem, that wispy idea, "A woman's place is in the home." Until we change that to "A woman's place is where she wants it," we will continue to read sad episodes like the one which opened this chapter:

"A TV reporter was chatting with some children not long ago, and turning to a little boy, he asked, 'What would you like to be when you grow up?' . . ."

Our granddaughters, and perhaps even our daughters, will no longer be willing to live only a life of mother or subordinate. It is projected that 22 percent more women will be in the work market this decade. They are going to want and need to work to preserve a shrinking, isolated planet. To do this, they will need a life-style with many facets—just as men have had for centuries.

Society declares that your "acceptable" place is "behind a man." But what will you do when there is no man to stand behind? What will you do when your free time becomes empty time? We all must shake ourselves free of mythical cobwebs and demand that we be treated as full citizens in our society. We must insist that our legislators pass laws freeing us to work if we want and as we want.

Let's hope that the anecdote of the reporter and the children will soon become an interesting bit of history instead of a timely news story.

13

The Morality
Of Selfishness

"What's happening to women today?" is the plaintive way entertainer Mike Douglas put it to me during an interview two years ago.

"What's happening" is more than a readjustment of human relationships. It's a revolution. To put it simply, women want the chance to realistically hope for the career and self-achievement rewards that men hope for. Yet this threatens so many people. It threatens older women who have accommodated themselves to the traditional path; they resent the "upstart rabble-rousers" who intimate that the time-venerated "right" life is suddenly all wrong. And it scares many men who are afraid to let the chicks out of their shells for fear they will commit some sort of "masculinity murder" (implying that without women to prop them up, they will collapse like undernourished tomato plants in July).

It would seem that these men have a rather empty masculine self-image, and are bent on squelching the feminist movement, making it another nostalgic vestige for historians in the next century to unearth and fit into the jigsaw puzzle of life in the 1970s. The afflicted men do this by twisting terms, like using "liberated" to denote the promiscuous paperdoll promised to every *Playboy* subscriber, and by revitalizing worn-out categories to settle us into, like "mad housewife" or "sensuous woman." Instead of being simply human beings, we are split up into the collaterals of teeny-bopper, nympho, mama, or granny. The thing we are credited with having in common is the proclivity to buy security and sex appeal through pantyhose and plastic gloves.

A woman has got to be pretty well together to stand up to these kinds of slurs, and self-assurance is one thing women have not been peddled. Quite the opposite. With our entrenched fear of not getting a man, or of losing the man we've got, we are often tossed like a volleyball from the fingers of guilt to the hands of doubt.

Usually, the most vociferous of those male slur-slingers can't take it themselves. Imply to such men that they aren't all their public image claims and they shudder with indignation before shriveling into impotency. Intimate that Joe Doe isn't quite Joe Namath (even if you're happy with him as he is), and old Joe is paralyzed.

We have been programmed to inflate the male ego with shots of proper female jealousy. Remember the story of the husband whose wife complains that he's always ogling other women? "When I stop looking," he warns the old lady, "*then* you'll have to worry." What he means, naturally, is when he's no longer interested in seducing *all* women, wife as well will be deprived of his sexual favors. On the other hand, let her do some eye-exercising herself, and hubby runs for the separation papers.

Admittedly, there are men today, actually walking and breathing (perhaps even in your own home), who are self-assured enough in their masculinity and in their humanity to accept women alongside and even ahead of them, rather than three steps behind. At this point in our cultural growth, however, they are not the vocal majority. Though certain economic and political pimps have grabbed headlines with panicked plans of attack on Women's Liberation, punctuated by derisive laughter, their nonexistent logic has failed to discredit the movement. Women are moving like pins toward a magnet, shaking away the outmoded rules and roles.

We are disputing the claim that, just because in the past feminine life-style has been embroidered with words like *passivity* and *docility*, these are the traits of every woman. Today, women in droves are rising up from their suburban split-levels, and tossing away natural childbirth and nursing as the *only* roads to female fulfillment.

We are discarding pay-less PTA and fund-raising as the *sole* means open to us for contributing to society. And we are looking within ourselves for what *we* want to do with our lives. For we realize that our responsibility is ultimately to ourselves and that accepting that responsibility is when selfishness becomes moral.

We have seen that past feminist movements have failed because women were *not* selfish; they were obliged to show some humanitarian justification for feminism, such as abolishing demon-rum or slavery. Woman was the personification of Devotion to (and I quote in order) Husband, Children, Church, and the Moral Aims of Society.

This is not femininity. It is slavery. There is no beauty in enforced serfdom where ideas are inculcated rather than self-determined. We women will only reach our respective goals of liberation by recognizing ourselves as people first, with the authentic human feelings of fear, vulnerability, toughness, love, and hate—in all combinations. Then perhaps we can shed the guilt feelings we have accumulated through the ages to protect us from ourselves.

To do this, we are waving farewell to being the providers of *male* necessities and are becoming partakers of *human* necessities. We want no more of that you-bring-in-the-money-and-I'll-spend-it contract and the division it automatically creates within a marriage. Life is simple, really—a warm bed, a hot meal, soothing words, and an attentive, caring companion. The only thing wrong is that, up to now, it's been feminine to provide and masculine to take the nonmaterial human portion of these essentials.

Today, we are recognizing ourselves as the most potentially powerful group that exists. The Census Bureau reports that almost half of us are working; in education, the number of college girls has increased 160 percent in the last decade. For every 104 million women there are 99 million men, so it is obvious that we are going to have to find some source of fulfillment and identity other than being a wife. A goodly number of gals are going to find themselves working alone and living alone, and they'd better learn not only to live with it, but to love it.

Culturally, modern woman is a different breed from women before her. She has been brought up alongside men and educated with men. She socializes with men more now than ever before. But aside from the role of comforter, woman's sole traditional activity today is full-time mother, and just as every woman is not mentally or physically equipped to be a professional rigger or a television producer, neither is every woman satisfied in the role of round-the-clock mom. Having babies just won't do it anymore. More and more women are admitting it and they find that, as a result, no thunder crashes and no bolt of lighting strikes them down. But, if culture, history, husbands, children, parents, employers, neighbors, government, and the communications industry have all teamed up to glorify us as society's handmaiden, what do we do about it?

One way to get moving is to take advantage of what the other minorities have learned, not only today's blacks, Puerto Ricans, and Indians but the Europeans before them. They learned that individuals do not lift themselves up alone. They form self-help groups, permeate businesses and professions, and finally take over what other groups have controlled. We women, too, must build up a coterie of physicians, lawyers, church leaders, and politicians with whom we and our children can identify, and erase impressions such as doctor equals man and nurse equals woman.

But this takes group support. Trying to make it alone won't work. When a woman reached a high professional level, she tended, in the past, to become a pseudo-man with all his guarded aggressions. There is a story about the old-line Roman Catholic who told the Pope John-oriented young priest, "We had to obey all those church rules when we were young. I don't like to see our children getting off so easy today." In a similar way, successful women often exclaimed, "I had to scratch and fight my way up. Let her do the same."

The reason for her struggle, of course, is that the career girl often had to play both sides of the game, masculine as well as feminine. On the masculine side, she tended to ridicule other women, especially the old-fashioned variety. On the feminine side, she had to catch hold of a rising man's coattails and let him pull her up after him; other women were potential competitors to be swatted away. We don't need any more of that.

Aside from organizing to achieve more, we need to start redefining ourselves without relying on male standards. "Femininity," for example, is going to vary from woman to woman. Hopefully, some of the traditional "female" characteristics will become more widely thought of as desirable "human" traits. In the past, Christ, Gandhi, and Martin Luther King were venerated for such "feminine" characteristics as passivity and gentility. These traits, however, were so threatening to the insecure male that their exponents had to be expelled with machismic violence.

The attempt to redefine such standard terms as *woman, feminine,* and *female* is the reason the phenomenon called consciousness-raising has taken such a hold within the Women's Liberation movement. It has been scoffed at in the press as some sort of group therapy, but consciousness-raising is more than medication since it is prescribed for healthy, "normal" women. A housewife, a career woman, a student can examine her own life, asking, "What is it like for me to live as a woman in a man's world?"

Each individual's experiences and resentments surface in response to other women's situations. Slowly you begin to realize that "womanly" behavior is an ideal, a reaction to a man—a husband, a father, a boss. A woman's "womanly behavior," or femininity, isn't the same with every man. It shifts focus, but always within the generally accepted idea of womanhood. And somehow you never quite live up to all the ideals.

Consciousness-raising offers new freedom. It also offers a new closeness. Most of us have enjoyed friendships with other women while growing up, in school, and at work. But much of the time, even the closest of these relationships had definite boundaries. What you confided in Marge, you didn't bring up with Sue. Even over intimate coffees at the kitchen table, there were just some things you never talked over with your next-door neighbor because "she isn't the type to understand," or "she'd be shocked," or "she'd just laugh." Yet, they were girl problems, and you were both girls.

And then there was always that final cutoff point when a man came into view. If you both had your eye on the new account executive, some element in your relationship was wrenched away. This competitiveness is activated not only by a specific man, but by men in general. We split away from our girl friends as we grow closer to the "feminine" ideal.

The woman next door dresses up nightly to greet her husband home from work, but it never crosses your mind to do the same until you drop in on her at 4:30 P.M. when she is stroking nail polish across her fingertips and you notice that yours are chewed to the skinline. Things like that inject a splinter into your friendship. Or when a friend finds endless things to do with chopped beef and the only hamburger variations you know are "with cheese" and "plain." These are the times guilt chisels a niche in your mind. You are competing with every other woman, usually for no reason other than guilt.

In these feminist, consciousness-raising groups, there is no need for ice-breaking, time-killing chitchat. No one asks, "What does your husband do?" or "How many children do you have?" unless it relates to your specific problem. If someone is hurt, frightened, or threatened at some point, there is comfort offered. A woman telling whatever is on her mind will know that the other women will understand, and, unlike her neighbor at home, will not disapprove.

The group will empathize when Cindy complains, "My kids bore me" or "I feel I'm a rotten mother," because they have accepted that, at times, their children bore them too, and that no woman lives up to the TV mother-goddess ideal. Suppose Helen admits, "I feel I have left my husband far behind me in my thinking. If he doesn't catch up, I don't know how I can continue with my marriage." Will such a marriage be saved for *not* having said these things? It can only be easier for Helen to know others will sympathize and will not berate her.

I spent close to a year in a consciousness-raising group. The effect was at first almost overwhelming. When I'd come home from a session, I couldn't sleep, I was so wrought up about my own revelations or someone else's. This intermingling of my life with other women's lives was a new and unique experience for me. It is very different from sharing a man's life, for in marriage, two people are building a life together. In a consciousness-raising group, individuals are not building something together, but helping each other to deal with life—as women and as people.

We encouraged each other to mention any topic. There were no taboos except in methods of discussion. For instance, one member had a habit of beginning, "This happened to a friend of mine . . ." or "I read about one woman who . . ." We discouraged this. The member, not the absent "friend," was important.

Also shunned was theorizing, such as "What do you think about Sigmund Freud's theory of the vaginal orgasm?" Freud's ideas are not valid topics in consciousness-raising. However, a member's personal feelings about vaginal orgasm are extremely relevant. A member can voice fears, frustrations, and humiliations, and no one will slough them off as symptoms of "that time of the month" for "the little woman."

Consciousness-raising groups vary in size, although my personal experience leads me to believe that six to nine members works best. Meeting every week keeps the continuity. No observers or visitors are allowed. From there on, each group takes on its own characteristics. At one gathering, everyone may sit on the floor, each member taking her turn to discuss specified topics for that evening. Another group may choose chairs around a dining room table, and discuss any subject that seems important that night.

In my group, topics arose in different ways. One evening, Jane announced, "I was on the bus this morning, and two men in the seat behind me verbally tore apart every woman in sight. I felt like a trapped animal and I felt every other woman was caught in the same trap." From there on, the group took over. Every member had something to add and something to take from that opener. Jane's incident was personal to her, and the other women, just by being women in this society, could relate to it.

The group can turn out to be fantastically supportive as well as quite threatening. Dredging up the workings of a mind is not a trivial chore. Doors may be shut as protection against guilt and injury, but there is still activity behind the shut doors. To begin facing the frustrations, turmoils, and upsets writhing within is often a treacherous undertaking.

It might be impossible to find "solutions," but

it is very possible for you, as a member, to gain enough support from other members to begin seeing yourself as more than "just a woman." You will accept yourself as a human being and you may gain enough confidence to demand more of yourself. What you definitely gain is the knowledge that other women have similar problems, and that no situation or experience is too intolerable for people to share.

Sounds dangerous? Any growth process begins from within and sometimes it hurts to expand, but while painful, it's exhilarating—not only for you but for all who've shared in your growth. From this root of consciousness-raising grows the strong stem of awakening and acceptance—and ultimately the flowering of women as people.

Once our consciousness has been raised, we can no longer blame anyone for keeping us buried. We can only pick up the shovel and start digging ourselves out. What kind of world will we have? Astrologer, I'm not, nor seer, nor prophet. One thing I can say though is that we won't be like men. We can't be, obviously, but neither do we want to be. We will be able to recognize and express our feelings, and we'll be able to help our children express what is inside them. They will respect their mother as a parent and adult, rather than viewing her as the biggest kid in the house, ever dependent upon daddy for an allowance and for permission to have that new dress. And through this, our sons and daughters can learn to respect each other.

And in marriage, what will Women's Liberation mean? Marriage is changing even without the prodding of feminism. Extended families and cluster families are beckoning in the alienated suburbs, just as communes are attracting the young. Hopefully, once we begin to recognize alternate life-styles, the quality of traditional marriage will be improved for those who choose that road.

Perhaps instituting renewal clauses in marriage contracts will help erase divorce guilt. The concept that a couple has failed if they have not achieved that ideal marriage will dissolve when we can accept marriage as a partnership of continuous growth and new experiences. The theory that a husband and wife can be everything to each other is unbelievably idealistic. Supporters of such a theory are doomed at best to resignation, a feeling that one makes the best of this precarious life. At worst, they give up. This leaves a divorced man who is deprived of sharing his children's growth and contributing to their development. And it leaves the ex-wife grasping bitterly for alimony and child support—all she can get—in a desperate effort to get even. For without a man, she is identity-less— nothing. She had been told long ago to give up her own goals. The price for this man was high.

Clare Booth Luce, in her satire of Henrik Ibsen's *A Doll's House,* estimated that a wife of ten years was deserving of approximately $53,000 severance pay for her work as full-time cook, cleaning woman, handyman, laundress, seamstress, part-time gardener, and chauffeur. This would include the husband's donation of rent, taxes, clothing, medical expenses, and food. No fringe benefits. No charge for sleeping with him.

Bitter? Yes, but a package of truth.

What, finally, will liberation mean to you and to

other women? I can say now that many women will no longer feel fulfillment only when baby eats a hearty supper and be doomed to hopelessness years later when that rotund offspring springs off on his own, leaving mother with an empty spoon and a barren life. After the years spent taking care of her family, a woman will no longer find herself useless. Her next thirty years will not be aimless, while her husband's career peaks and her children pursue their lives. Not with the crying need for more competent government leaders, physicians, and caring people in all fields and not when today's world demands a change of priorities, and fast! Many of these new priorities, such as a concern for the welfare of people, will emerge out of the "feminine attitude" always before used to support men.

This "feminine attitude" is not a weakness but a strength. We women are strong, but we have stifled our strength to play Pretty Petunia. Studies show that women withstood the traumatic London blitz far better than did the men. Some of our so-called inherited female traits could be put to good use outside the narrow family environment in the wide world of pollution, consumer fraud, war, natural disasters, and disease. I would never presume to say women will make a heaven on earth. However, we sure couldn't do any worse than what's been done in the past—and what's being done now.

Again, we must first clear away that mythology which we accepted and wove into a way of life. We must stop accepting manufacturers' astronomically high prices for cosmetics, after their advertising has subliminally convinced us that without smeary moist lipstick we will be drab asexuals. Or stockings which run if you look at them sharply, but which are as important to our attire as a wool coat in winter. When the midi appeared, women shouted, "No, not for me!" and they went out and bought pants suits which, after all, served the same purpose of boosting the fashion economy.

We want to do our share in halting pollution, but, when we go to purchase bio-degradable detergents and food without additives, we find the prices so high that we must continue to use the damaging products—but with a new burden of guilt. (Women don't need that!)

All this does not mean that those of us who love creating a fondue or stitching a cover for the footstool must feel that the traditional niceties will disappear. Here again, we come back to choice. A woman's role is going to be whatever she chooses to make it, and donning a spacesuit will be no more threatening to her femininity than stitching a spring suit. What is being changed is the stereotype, not the people. A woman is feminine because she is a woman, and whether or not she teases her hair or bakes the daily bread has nothing to do with it.

Okay, so "Bitch, Sister, Bitch" still sounds too bitchy for you. But how does this sound: "We must look upon the female character as being a sort of natural deficiency," and "Bound to serve, love and obey"? Visions of amiable idiots in chains dance from these words.

It's all going to change, so start preparing your man your way. Start changing your children's images of themselves and of you. If it's your hand that rocks the cradle and rules the world, it's also your selfishness that can change the world.

Back again to the question, What do we want? More than "equal pay for equal work," though incredibly we still have that to gain. We want a chance for a full partnership in life, competing *with* men and not *for* men. We want to be equal to men, not the same as men. And we want to fit into a life that often looks like a jigsaw puzzle with many pieces missing. Perhaps we can fit into those vital spaces and give the time we live in some special meaning. And yes, we do want to be feminine, but in our own way. For feminine is human, that's all.

One day, a woman from a nearby suburb telephoned me to ask when the next meeting of our women's group was scheduled. I told her. She was obviously interested, but seemed hesitant about actually attending.

"Tell me what you look like," I urged, "so I'll know you when you arrive. Every month we get several newcomers."

After a few silent seconds she said, "Well, I'm over forty . . ."

Over forty. That, unfortunately, is how women have been conditioned to think of themselves. If she were young and confident, she would have described herself as "medium-height, blond . . ." But "over forty" seemed to say "because I am no longer youthful, I have no chance to be attractive, useful, or even worth noticing."

Let's hope these denigrating self-images will disintegrate. However, let's not fool ourselves into believing they will self-destruct. It is we who must lift ourselves up.

It's happening already. A Roman Catholic theologian was quoted recently as telling anthropologist Margaret Mead, "I am an individual human being. I have nothing to give that's unique to my sex."

If it takes a revolution to recognize that, then perhaps it's time.

Epilogue:
One Last Question...

Several months ago, my wife and I were leaving the theater in New York City, and while walking down Broadway, I spotted a burly guy striding toward us. As we approached each other, he deliberately lowered his shoulder and knocked into me. I continued on, but he came after me and tapped me on the shoulder.

"Hey, Pal," he said, "you gotta be more careful when you're walking. Things like that can get you into bad trouble."

"I don't think I walked into you," I replied, "but if I did, please excuse me."

A crowd was gathering. "You're not calling me a

225

liar," he yelled, adding invectives and obscenities with mounting hysteria.

I answered, "Excuse me," and we walked away.

It wasn't until we reached the next street that I appreciated what really happened. I wasn't embarrassed. I didn't feel cowardly. But was this typical of my behavior? Ten years ago I would have gotten into an altercation at such a challenge. But now it was different. I didn't feel any need to prove my "machismo."

Surprisingly, a different situation developed some weeks later when our daughter, Jeannine, then seven, came home from school one afternoon. She was crying because Billy was always hitting her after classes.

"That's silly," I responded. "How can a little guy hurt you when you're a year and a half older and much bigger and stronger?"

But when Jeannine insisted that my wife accompany her home from school as "security," I thought it would be worth a try to teach her a bit of self-defense.

I explained that fighting is not the best way to argue, but sometimes it comes in handy. It was proven to her the next time Billy tried to have some "fun"; Jeannine's one short punch to the mid-section sent him home and caused a remarkable metamorphosis from insecurity to confidence in our daughter.

Of course, I am not preaching violence but rather suggesting that the traditional rigid roles assigned to men and women are passé. Yet, most facets of our society reflect sexism: Once, my young son asked me what my favorite soft drink was.

"Like," I answered.

"But dad, *Like*'s made just for girls!" he complained, repeating the popular advertisement at that time.

Trying to eliminate girl-boy roles just in our *family* can be a tough job. Very recently, Jeannine, Jason, and a friend's son were playing hospital. The two boys were surgeons, and Jeannine was the nurse.

"Why aren't you all doctors?" I asked.

"I never saw a woman doctor," Jeannine answered.

"There are no woman doctors," her friend declared. "Not even on television."

My wife and I realized that no matter how forceful our ideas may be, the media and the peer groups are barriers we must constantly combat. It means finding a female pediatrician for our children: it means making an effort to point out the women who are succeeding in "male" fields; it means making a series of small first steps.

It's not going to be easy to discard society's sexist attitudes. Next time you go into a doctor's office, pick up one of the medical journals and check out the advertisements of the drug companies. More often than not, you'll notice that women are the insomniacs, get the tension headaches, and suffer from the aging process. The female is the chronic complainer who needs medical help, implying that the male has no fifth decade hang-ups.

I'll admit that it's dreary to vacuum the living room rug just because I'm home that day and it has to be done. How convenient it would be to claim, "Vacuuming is your job, dear, and after you're finished, why don't you fix me a hot pastrami on rye with an ice cold beer?" Convenient, yes, but not really honest.

Recently, at a dinner party, the conversation was moving along amiably enough when one of the guests remembered that my wife is actively involved in the women's rights movement. Suddenly the atmosphere became hostile. Women stiffened their shoulders defensively, and husbands smirked knowingly. One engineer remarked, "You must have some hang-ups. Any man who lets his wife get involved with those freaks couldn't be all man."

Actually, I feel a great weight off my shoulders having a relationship with my wife which is not based on my keeping her supplied with midis, minis, and makeup. To be sure, I am speaking only of our marriage, and in fact, my viewpoint of it. I am happy to know that my wife will be fulfilled even after our children are grown, continuing her present career or tackling another challenge.

I am speaking also for our daughter, satisfied that passage of the Equal Rights Amendment will mean equal rights for her as a female citizen; she will not be discriminated against in entrance requirements to state universities; when she marries, she will no longer be barred in many states from conducting business affairs, selling property, or attaining loans in her own name.

As for our son, he can study mechanical arts and home economics if he chooses. He will hopefully not shoulder the weight of unfair alimony and child-support if he marries and then separates. And, probably, the burden of bearing arms for this country will no longer be placed on male backs alone.

In short, our children can stand as equal, responsible, and contributing citizens under the law. To me, this current demand for women's rights is a demand for dignity, another aspect of the whole battle for human rights and individual self-definition.

One last question left in my mind now is, How come it took so long?

Acknowledgments

The author wishes to acknowledge and thank the following persons and organizations for their permissions to reprint:

Shana Alexander and *McCalls Magazine* for material on page 189, from "Where the Women Are" by Shana Alexander, *McCalls*, February 1971; American Baby, Inc. for material on pages 186-90, from "Day-Care, What Does It Mean?" by Elizabeth Anticaglia, *Mothers-To-Be, American Baby*, October 1971; Catherine Drinker Bowen and Harold Ober Associates, Inc. for material on page 186, from "We've Never Asked a Woman Before" by Catherine Drinker Bowen, *Atlantic*, March 1970, Reprinted with permission of Harold Ober Associates Incorporated, Copyright © 1970 by Catherine Drinker Bowen; Cadwell Davis Company, Inc., New York, and *TV GUIDE®* Magazine for material on pages 40 and 47, from "Is Television Making a Mockery of the American Woman?" by Edith Efron, *TV GUIDE®*, August 8, 1970, Copyright © 1970 by Triangle Publications, Inc., Radnor, Pa., Reprinted with permission from *TV GUIDE®* Magazine; Coronet Magazine for the material on pages 57-58, from "The Changing Look of Sex" by Elizabeth Anticaglia, *Coronet*, November 1970, Coronet Communications, Inc., New York, N. Y.; Houghton Mifflin Company for material on page 184, from *Unbought and Unbossed* by Shirley Chisholm, Houghton Mifflin Company, Boston, 1971, pp. 114, 167; Alfred A. Knopf, Inc. for material on page 125, from *The Second Sex* by Simone de Beauvoir, Alfred A. Knopf, Inc., New York, p. 48, Copyright © 1951 by Alfred A. Knopf, Inc.; Anne Koedt for material on pages 140-41, from "The Myth of the Vaginal Orgasm," *Notes From the Second Year*, 1970, pp. 37-38; Little, Brown and Company for material on pages 136 and 141, from *Understanding Human Sexual Inadequacy* by Fred Belliveau and Lin Richter, Little, Brown and Company, Publishers, Boston, 1970; David McKay Company, Inc. for material on page 158, from *Born Female* by Caroline Bird, David McKay Company, Inc., New York, 1971; The Macmillan Company for material on pages 124, 157, and 159-60, from

The Natural Superiority of Women (Revised Edition) by Ashley Montagu, The Macmillan Company, New York, 1970, Copyright © 1945, 1953, 1968 by Ashley Montagu; Medical Tribune Inc. for material on pages 91-92, from "N.Y. Committee Finds Girls Able to Play on Boy's Teams," *Medical Tribune*, March 24, 1971; *Medical World News* for material on pages 117-18 and 205, from "Women MD's Join the Fight," *Medical World News*, October 23, 1970; Newsweek, Inc. for material on pages 186-90, from "Day Care: The Boom Begins," *Newsweek*, December 7, 1970, Copyright Newsweek, Inc.; *New York Magazine* for the quote on page 108, from an interview by Diana Lurie, *New York*, August 31, 1970, p. 29; W. W. Norton and Company, Inc. for the material on pages 40-41 and 167-68, from *The Feminine Mystique* by Betty Friedan, W. W. Norton and Company, Inc., New York, 1963, Copyright © 1963 by Betty Friedan, Reprinted with permission of the publisher; Quadrangle Books, Inc. for the material on pages 174-75, from *Everyone Was Brave* by William O'Neill, Quadrangle Books, Inc., Chicago, 1969, pp. 352-53; Alice S. Rossi and The Atlantic Monthly Company for material on page 195, from "Job Discrimination and What Women Can Do About It" by Alice S. Rossi, *Atlantic*, March 1970, Copyright © 1970 by The Atlantic Monthly Company, Boston, Reprinted with permission; Gloria Steinem and *McCalls Magazine* for material on page 61, from "What Playboy Doesn't Know About Women. . . . ." by Gloria Steinem, *McCalls*, October 1970; *TV GUIDE®* *Magazine* for material on pages 40, 45, 47, and 49-50, from "Is Television Making a Mockery of the American Woman?" by Edith Efron, *TV GUIDE®*, August 8, 1970, Copyright © 1970 by Triangle Publications, Inc., Radnor, Pa., Reprinted with permission from *TV GUIDE®* *Magazine;* Women on Words and Images for the material on pages 77-78, from "Sex Stereotypes in Elementary School Readers," Women on Words and Images, 25 Cleveland Lane, R.D. #4, Princeton, N.J., 08540.

The author also wishes to acknowledge the following:

"Adam's Rib, or the Woman Within" by Una Stannard, *Trans-Action*, November-December 1970; "A Doll's House" by Clare Booth Luce, *Life*, October 16, 1970; "Female Biology in a Male Culture" by Diana Trilling, *Saturday Review*, October 10, 1970; *The History of Woman Suffrage*, vol. 1, *Declaration of Sentiments and Resolutions* by Elizabeth C. Stanton et al.; "Militants for Women's Rights" by Sara Davidson, *Life*, December 12, 1969; *New York Times*, January 31, 1971, April 25, 1971, May 9, 1971, and October 31, 1971 issues; *The Prisoner of Sex* by Norman Mailer, Boston, Little, Brown and Company, 1971; "A Unique Competence: A study of equal employment opportunity in the Bell System," Equal Employment Opportunities Commission, Washington, D.C., 1971; "What Is Sex Appeal?" by Leon Salzman, MD, *Medical Aspects of Human Sexuality*, April 1970; "Woman Today" (a weekly column) by Elizabeth Anticaglia, *Today's Post*, Montgomery Publishing Company, Pa.